Study Guide

for

Stojkovic, Klofas and Kalinich's

Criminal Justice Organizations
Administration and Management

Second Edition

Paul Katsampes
Metropolitan State College of Denver

West/Wadsworth
I(T)P® An International Thomson Publishing Company

Belmont, CA • Albany, NY • Bonn • Boston • Cincinnati • Detroit • Johannesburg • London
Madrid • Melbourne • Mexico City • New York • Paris • Singapore • Tokyo • Toronto • Washington

COPYRIGHT © 1998 by Wadsworth Publishing Company
A Division of International Thomson Publishing Inc.
I(T)P® The ITP logo is a registered trademark under license.

Printed in the United States of America
1 2 3 4 5 6 7 8 9 10

For more information, contact Wadsworth Publishing Company, 10 Davis Drive, Belmont, CA 94002, or electronically at http://www.thomson.com/wadsworth.html

International Thomson Publishing Europe
Berkshire House 168-173
High Holborn
London, WC1V 7AA, England

International Thomson Editores
Campos Eliseos 385, Piso 7
Col. Polanco
11560 México D.F. México

Thomas Nelson Australia
102 Dodds Street
South Melbourne 3205
Victoria, Australia

International Thomson Publishing Asia
221 Henderson Road
#05-10 Henderson Building
Singapore 0315

Nelson Canada
1120 Birchmount Road
Scarborough, Ontario
Canada M1K 5G4

International Thomson Publishing Japan
Hirakawacho Kyowa Building, 3F
2-2-1- Hirakawacho
Chiyoda-ku, Tokyo 102, Japan

International Thomson Publishing GmbH
Königswinterer Strasse 418
53227 Bonn, Germany

International Thomson Publishing Southern Africa
Building 18, Constantia Park
240 Old Pretoria Road
Halfway House, 1685 South Africa

All rights reserved. No part of this work covered by the copyright hereon may be reproduced or used in any form or by any means—graphic, electronic, or mechanical, including photocopying, recording, taping, or information storage and retrieval systems—without the written permission of the publisher.

ISBN 0-534-21416-9

Study Guide

for

Stojkovic, Klofas and Kalinich's

Criminal Justice Organizations
Administration and Management

CRIMINAL JUSTICE ORGANIZATIONS: ADMINISTRATION AND MANAGEMENT
Second Edition

Table of Contents

Part I	The Nature Of Criminal Justice Organizations		1
	Chapter 1	Basic Concepts For Understanding Criminal Justice Organizations	1
	Chapter 2	Structure Of Criminal Justice Organizations	4
	Chapter 3	The Criminal Justice System In Its Environment	13
Part II	The Individual in Criminal Justice Organizations		
	Chapter 4	Problems of Communication	21
	Chapter 5	Motivation of Personnel	27
	Chapter 6	Job Design	37
	Chapter 7	Leadership	41
	Chapter 8	Personnel Supervision And Evaluation	50
Part III	Group Behavior in Criminal Justice Organizations		
	Chapter 9	Occupational Socialization	58
	Chapter 10	Power And Political Behavior	68
	Chapter 11	Organizational Conflict	76
Part IV	Processes in Criminal Justice Organizations		
	Chapter 12	Decision Making	82
	Chapter 13	Organizational Effectiveness	91
	Chapter 14	Change and Innovation	97
	Chapter 15	Research In Criminal Justice Organizations	113

Appendices

Appendix A - Correctional Leadership Instrument	A-1
Appendix B - Team Project Materials	B-1
Appendix C - Test Bank	C-1

Course Strategy

This manual has been designed to assist professors and students use the text, Criminal Justice Organizations: Administration and Management, 2nd.,ed. as completely as possible. The chapter summaries, chapter objectives, key terms, and chapter outlines have been organized to facilitate readers to quickly focus on the essential elements of each chapter. These study and presentation tools are not intended to replace reading the text. The parts of the text that have not been included in the study tools are the criminal justice examples and management discussions that the reader needs to really understand the text authors' rich examination of these management and organization principles and techniques.

The content of this manual supports the approach that the class should be examined and processed as an emerging organization in itself. The students and faculty may work together to make the organization (class) productive and successful. To gain from the experience of the class as an organization, the instructor should periodically process the organizational behavior of the class including the instructor's management style and its effects on the class members. It is the instructor's responsibility to create a learning environment and it is the students' responsibility to learn by reading, relating to examples, and experiencing through participation in projects.

The exercises at the end of each chapter and the multiple choice test bank questions and answers allow the class participants the opportunity to evaluate their understanding of the text content. The test banks in the instructor's guide and the student manual similar but not identical.

The team project materials are provided to allow for the development of class group projects by students. The questionnaire in these materials is a guide for analyzing and organization. Because positive group behavior is critical to the success of organizations, creating a team project is recommended. When the team project objectives include analyzing a criminal justice agency, the opportunity to learn the principles of organizational behavior and the practice of management is expanded greatly.

The purpose of this text, manual and course is to increase the effectiveness and productivity of criminal justice organizations. When organizations improve the personal and professional development of the practitioners is increased. With this objective in mind, the appropriate use of this manual becomes important. If a user of this manual requires further assistance or support please contact the author.

Paul Katsampes, DPA
    303.556.8153 telephone
    303.556.5357 fax
    pkatsampes @ AOL.com

Part I—The Nature of Criminal Justice Organizations

Chapter 1
Basic Concepts for Understanding Criminal Justice Organizations

Chapter Overview

Organizations are a significant part of our lives. We are immersed early in schools and scouting, churches and athletic teams. We continue in colleges and universities, military service, employment, and our organized social life. This immersion in organizations continues throughout our lives, and, in the end, our obituaries will include a chronicle of our organizational attachments.

Among the many organizations that touch our lives are those of the criminal justice system. Many Americans will be only indirectly involved in these organizations. They may find themselves fighting a traffic ticket in court or touring the local jail while serving on a grand jury. Other Americans will find themselves immersed in the criminal justice system when they are processed as offenders. Still others will be employees of criminal justice organizations.

Our ties to organizations differ, as do the size, structure, and purpose of those organizations. The analysis of those differences forms a large part of organizational research and theory, from which this book draws. Our approach to this material is eclectic. We do not intend either to introduce a new organizational theory as it applies to criminal justice or to reflect any single theoretical perspective in this book. Instead, our goal is to provide an overview of organizational theory and research as it applies to criminal justice.

We cannot proceed, however, without devoting special attention to some key theoretical concepts and ideas. In this chapter we define and describe those that have come to be widely accepted and that we feel are necessary as a foundation for the study of criminal justice administration and management.

Learning Objectives
When finished studying this chapter the reader will be able to:
1. Define three major elements of an organization.
2. Define management.
3. Define the major differences between open system theory and closed system theory.
4. Define leadership.
5. Define the issues of meeting organizational goals.
6. List four examples of a complex environment.

Key Terms

Organization	Complex Environment	Socialization
Management	Internal Constituencies	Complex Goals
Leadership	Structure	Bureaucracies
Open System	Activities	Policy
Closed System	Purpose	Unionization

Chapter Outline

I. What Is an Organization?
    A. Structure
        1. Weber's Bureaucratic Model (1947)
            a. Clear division of labor
            b. Formal rules
            c. Rigid hierarchy of offices
        2. Barnard's (1938) - " Organization is system of consciously coordinated activities or forces of two or more persons."
    B. Purpose
        1. Etzioni's Definition - Organizations are social units deliberately constructed and reconstructed to achieve certain goals.
        2. Organizations have many goals and they are often conflicting.
    C. Activities
        1. Socialization of employees affects activities
        2. Activities are managed by decision making

II. What Is Management?
    A. Carlisle (1976) - "The process by which the elements of a group are integrated, coordinated ad utilized to effectively and efficiently achieve the organization's objectives"
    B. May be associated with a particular office
    C. Top managers, mid-level managers, and first line supervisors are all management

III. What is Leadership?
    A. Kotter (1990) "Leadership refers to a process that helps direct and mobilize people and their ideas."
        1. Leadership is tribal in nature.
        2. Managers focus on planning, budgeting, setting short term goals, and procedures.
        3. Leaders establish a futures vision.
        4. Leaders challenge existing processes and systems.

        5. They create change and practice the art of statesmanship.
    B. Criminal Justice mangers have assumed they work in a closed system.
        1. Closed system controls its environment.
        2. Communication follows lines of authority.
        3. Power and authority are a function of the office.
        4. Change is slow and directed by management.

IV. Open-System Theory
    A. Katz and Kahn (1978) describe organizations as open systems characterized by inputs from the environment. Throughput (the process of changing those inputs), and outputs (the product or service of an organization).
    B. Organizations have a selection process that determines how it deals with the environment.

V. Complex Goals
    A. Simon (1964) - Organizations have multiple and conflicting goals
        1. Organizations must work to meet all goals.
        2. Several goals may be met simultaneously.
    B. Goals provide direction and they serve as limits and constraints
        1. Goal conflict may promote efficiency.

VI. Complex Environment
    A. Lipsky (1980) - States that the conflicting goals organizations are the result of unresolved disagreements in society at large.
    B. Criminal justice organizations are still designed along para military lines which indicates focus as a closed system.

VII. Complex Internal Constituencies
    A. There is an internal struggle for power in organizations.
    B. Work force is major internal constituency.

Exercise

Students: prepare discussion of what is an organization? (Structure, Purpose, Activities) Answer the following question <u>yes or no</u> and support you choice with text references:

Are people on a beach an organization ?

Chapter 2
Structure of Criminal Justice Organizations

Chapter Overview

Organizations have a purpose, a structure, and activities. Organizations are also comprised of a formal structure and an informal structure. This phenomena was recognized by Chester Barnard in the 1940s: "Formal organizations arise out of and are necessary to informal organizations; but when they come into operation, they create and require informal organizations" (Barnard, 1948, p. 120). This book examines, to a great extent, the forces that impact criminal justice organizations and nurture the informal side of organizations. It is important, therefore to review for the reader the formal side of organizations to set the stage for the following chapters. This chapter provides the reader with a micro level description of the basic structures and dimensions of organizations, and describes the logic of various structural configurations that can be implemented by agencies. In addition, the chapter reviews the basic concepts of organizational <u>mission</u>, <u>policies</u>, <u>procedures</u>, and practices. Finally, the informal side of organizations are briefly discussed. Throughout the chapter, the concepts of organizational structure are applied to criminal justice agencies.

Criminal justice organizations vary greatly in terms of size and structure. The vast majority of criminal justice agencies in the United States are relatively small and serve suburban and rural communities. At the other extreme, cities like New York or Los Angeles command rather large and complex criminal justice systems. The Federal Bureau of Prisons is a massive organization with maximum, medium and security institutions across the United States. The Federal system also includes six metropolitan correctional centers (jails) located in major cities in the country. The Los Angeles County Jail system houses about 23,000 inmates, more than many states incarcerate. Again, at the other extreme, the Marquette County Jail, Marquette Michigan, has an inmate capacity of 50. It can easily be envisioned that a plethora of criminal justice agencies at the federal, state, county and municipal jurisdictions of varying sizes and complexity exist on some hypothetical continuum between the very large and small agencies. It is not possible to describe an organizational structure generic to all or most organizations. However, there are key dimensions that seem integral to almost all organizations regardless of size or structure. This chapter will provide a general description of organizational dimensions common to organizations and apply, through example, how different organizational structures can fit criminal justice agencies. The discussion will begin with a general description of two distinct models of organizations: The closed system model, most commonly referred to as Bureaucratic, mechanistic, formal, hierarchical etc., and the open system model alternately referred to as organistic, professional or informal.

Henry (1975) provides a sound sketch and comparison of both models. Bureaucracies - the closed system model - are predicated upon stable environmental conditions that create routine demands for services. Tasks, therefore, tend to be specialized and divided among the labor force. That is, each member of the organization will have a narrow range of duties that contributes to the overall mission of the agency. Means, or process are emphasized over outcomes. It is assumed that if everyone does their task correctly, the final product will naturally appear. In this regard, everyone's job is spelled out clearly with a formal job description which also dictates and limit's the amount of authority and responsibility an individual will have. Bureaucracies tend to be hierarchical, having a chain of command with authority and responsibility being delegated from the central authority downward.

Learning Objectives

When finished studying this chapter the reader will be able to:

1. Define three major differences between the open system and the closed system.
2. Define hierarchical and organistic.
3. Define the major differences between organizations that are centralized and that are decentralized.
4. Discuss the differences between line and staff personnel.
5. Define organizational mission, policy, and procedure.
6. List four examples of the informal organization.

Key Terms

Bureaucratic
Hierarchical
Closed System
Task Specialization
Span of Control
Complexity
Mission
Informal communications network
Informal leadership
Human Resource Frame
Symbiotic Frame

Formal
Organistic
Open System
Formalization
Centralization v. Decentralization
Allocation of Personnel
Policies and Procedures
Informal work groups
Structural Frame
Political Frame
Participative Management

Chapter Outline

I. Introduction: Overview of Organizational Structure
    A. Basic Concepts
        1. Mission
        2. Policies
        3. Procedures
        4. Practices
    B. Criminal Justice Organizations
        1. Vary in size and structure
        2. No generic structure
        3. There are key dimensions
    C. Two Distinct Models
        1. Closed System
            a. Bureaucratic
            b. Mechanistic
            c. Formal
            d. Hierarchical
        2. Open System
            a. Organistic
            b. Professional
            c. Informal
    D. Closed System
        1. Purpose
            a. Stable environment
            b. Routine demands for service
        2. Characteristics
            a. Workers have a narrow range of duties
            b. Process emphasized over outcomes
            c. Formal job descriptions
            d. Clear authority and responsibility
            e. Structure is hierarchical
            f. Authority and responsibility delegated from central authority
            g. Communications flows vertically
            h. Reliance on written rules and regulations
            i. Promotion based on subjective assessment and longevity
            j. Rigid chain of command
        3. Examples
            a. Large metropolitan law enforcement agencies
            b. Federal Bureau of Prisons
    E. Open System
        1. Purpose
            a. Unstable environment

        b. Non-routine demands for service
    2. Characteristics
        a. Tasks are not specialized
        b. Ends emphasized over means
        c. Tasks by groups and teams sharing expertise
        d. Shared authority and responsibility
        e. Structure is informal
        f. Authority and responsibility emanates from work groups
        g. Communications flows horizontally
        h. Reliance on general policy statements
        i. Leadership style focuses on coaching and advising
    3. Examples
        a. Small law enforcement agencies with less than 10 staff
        b. Research and planning departments

II. Dimensions of Organizational Structure
    A. Basic Elements
        1. Task Specialization
        2. Formalization
        3. Span of Control
        4. Centralization v. Decentralization
        5. Complexity
        6. Allocation of Personnel
    B. Task Specialization
        1. Dividing the work into smaller tasks
        2. High task specialization means worker performs a narrow range of activities
        3. Low task specialization means worker performs a wide range of activities
        4. Criminal justice agencies will have both high and low task specialization
        5. Law enforcement divides tasks by function
    C. Formalization
        1. High degree of formalization:
            a. will result in rules for most aspects of the work
            b. reduces uncertainty
            c. defines authority and decision making
        2. Low degree of formalization:
            a. requires high level of expertise
            b. subordinate high latitude and authority in decision making
            c. low dependency on written rules and regulations
    D. Span of Control
        1. Span of control is the number of employees reporting to a

supervisor
      2. Span of control depends on organization size, tasks, and skills of employees
      3. Narrow span is a low number of employees reporting to a supervisor
      4. Narrow span results in a tall hierarchy with numerous supervision levels
      5. Wide span of control is a large number of employees reporting to a supervisor
      6. Wide span of control results in a flat hierarchy with few supervision levels
   E. Centralization v. Decentralization
      1. Centralization indicates many decisions made by managers
      2. Centralization promotes control and predictability
      3. Decentralization indicates many participative decisions made by employees
      4. Decentralization promotes employees commitment to decision results
   F. Complexity
      1. Vertical complex organizational structures have a high number of levels
      2. Horizontal complex organizational structures have a high number of sub-units
   G. Allocation of Personnel
      1. Line personnel are responsible for the delivery of services
      2. Staff personnel are support staff

III. Mission, Policy, and Procedures
   A. Mission
      1. Provides the agency's purpose, goals, and objectives
      2. Molds activities, provides principles and values
      3. Serves as an anchor or direction
      4. Must be supported by individual values, beliefs and behaviors
      5. Derived from legislation, professional standards, and community values
   B. Policies and Procedures
      1. Directly connected to the mission
      2. Policies provide a statement of purpose action and rationale
      3. Procedures are step by step lists of activities
      4. Civil litigation usually begins with review of policies and procedures
      5. Agencies need to ensure that mission, policies, and procedures are followed

IV. Informal Structures in Organizations
　　A. Goals, activities or structures that do not appear "on paper"
　　　　1. A manifestation of the organizational culture
　　　　2. Depends on administrators ability to control behaviors of staff
　　B. Informal communications network
　　　　1. Communications through chain of command is inefficient
　　　　2. Every organization has "rumor mill" or "grapevine"
　　　　3. Information moves quickly vertically across working units
　　C. Informal work group
　　　　1. Individuals develop informal work groups to solve problems
　　　　2. They are productive if thy work toward organizational goals
　　D. Informal leadership
　　　　1. Informal leaders have power because of expertise or communications abilities
　　　　2. Informal leaders emerge to provide members with direction and structure

V. Organizational Frames
　　A. Conceptual approach to organizations more in-depth compared to formal and informal
　　　　1. Structural frame
　　　　2. Human resource frame
　　　　3. Political frame
　　　　4. Symbiotic frame
　　B. Structural Frame
　　　　1. See previous discussions concerning organizational structure.
　　C. Human Resource Frame
　　　　1. Based on premise that individuals have feelings, needs, and prejudices.
　　　　2. The key to effectiveness is to tailor organizations to people
　　　　3. Most theories of motivation are based on this frame.
　　　　4. Criminal justice bureaucracies are criticized for lacking ability to motivate staff.
　　D. Political Frame
　　　　1. Interest groups compete for scarce resources.
　　　　2. Unions demonstrate effectiveness of use of political power.
　　　　3. Informal leaders with political clout emerge as effective leaders.
　　　　4. Informal leaders can resist attempts of organizational change.
　　E. Symbiotic Frame
　　　　1. Organizations are driven more by rituals: Stories, heroes, and myths than by rules or management decisions.
　　　　2. Problems arise when actors play out their parts poorly and symbols lose their potency.

Exercise

Instructor: Form the class into small groups (3-6 persons per group) and have them answer the questions following the case. Allow the students 20 to 25 minutes for preparation to report out their findings. As the groups report facilitate discussions that relate to the chapter objectives, key words and the outline. The case is in the text in Chapter 2.

Case Study - Pine Mountain County

Pine Mountain County was in the process of building a new jail. The jail population had been steadily increasing and had reached a population of almost two thousand inmates. It was an old jail that had been annexed twice and had a rated population of nine hundred inmates. A decision was made to build a "new generation" jail. Bonnie Smith was slated to be the jail administrator. Bonnie had worked in corrections for over 15 years as a social worker and social work supervisor. Her intense work and dedication in planning the new jail, as well as her corrections back ground earned her the appointment, although many suspected her gender was the key determinant. The old jail had been run along traditional bureaucratic lines. Everyone was used to a chain of command, taking orders and avoiding responsibility. Bonnie believed in the new generation jail philosophy, which was contrary to the traditional way of running the jail, and change presented a number of exciting obstacles. Her enthusiasm was fueled by the challenges ahead. She had a fairly clear notion of reactions staff would have toward the new generation jail management philosophy. She was prepared.

Bonnie called a staff meeting of key personnel, which included command staff, union representatives, medical staff and social service personnel. She presented the mission of the new jail and the management philosophy. She explained that the overriding mission of the jail would be to ensure that inmates were not harmed physically, medically or psychologically as a result of their jail experience. The medical and social service staff nodded in agreement while the corrections staff exhibited strained facial responses. She then added that to carry out the mission, inmates would have to be controlled and to do so, the corrections officer would be considered the corner stone of the operation. The corrections staff looked surprised and the "professional' staff appeared quizzical.

"The CO," she explained "would be given the tools and discretion to run his or her unit." A lieutenant from the command staff replied:" "These officers must follow policies and procedures. They can't have any discretion. We tell them how to handle inmates."

"Not any more, Bonnie explained. "COs are going to be fully trained, as is everyone else in this jail. Shift sergeants and other command staff will act as coaches, advisors and communicators and will back up COs decisions as long as the decisions are legitimate."

A sergeant asked: "You mean COs are going to be able to decide when inmates will be punished?"
"Yes within limits, and when they will be rewarded. And, as long as they were within their limits, no one will counter man their decisions." Looking at the social service staff she added: "If an officer locks down an inmate for a day, or takes away visitation or phone privileges, you folks will not interfere in that decision."

The social service staff had always had almost complete prerogatives in dealing with inmates. An experienced social worker and a friend of Bonnie's asked: "But, if in my opinion, a change of the inmates status is important to his or her treatment, I will be allowed to change the COs decision, correct?"

Bonnie was prepared for his question. "In a word John, no. You can discuss the case with the officer and with his or her sergeant. But the general rule is that the CO will have the final say."

"What about a medical problem ?" a nurse asked.

"You will have authority in emergencies." Bonnie explained." But the fact is COs are on the front line and they will be the ones to spot emergencies, both medical and psychological. They will be summoning both the medical and social service staff for support. Let me state again, The CO is the corner stone of the jail. Everything we do is to support and serve the CO staff. We work for them."

"That is nuts." came bolting out of the mouth of a shift lieutenant. "These bozos don't know a medical problem from their you know what. If we didn't stay on top of them this jail would be in a shambles."

Bonnie was prepared for this bit of enthusiastic criticism." If you look at the assaults, attempted escapes, suicides, and documented rapes over the years, if you listen to the noise level, look at the broken down and filthy condition of this jail, I would say this jail is a shambles. COs follow procedures, but inmates do what ever they want. That is coming to end and we are going to run this jail, not the inmates. And it will be done by giving the COs professional status. They will be given the tools, training, discretion and support from all of us to do their job."

A seasoned Sergeant grinned and verified Bonnie's description of the jail. "You are right about the jail Bonnie. I don't know if your system will work. But all we do is keep inmates from escaping. They do what ever else they want to. The only COs that have some control violate the jail policies routinely. And, by the way, the rest of the COs couldn't tell a jail policy from their you know what."

The union representative applauded. "God bless you Bonnie. I hope you can pull it off. If you provide training and status to the COs, you will have my support."

Ellen from the social work staff joined the dissenters. "And you have just degraded my status and the status of all of the social service staff. We supported you for this appointment. That was a big mistake. We all have degrees and most have Masters Degrees in Social Work. Now you telling us the COs will have more to say about inmates than we will. This is an out rage. I am sending my resume out tomorrow."

"Good luck" Bonnie thought. The fun was just beginning.

Case Study Questions

1. To what extent is Bonnie forming a partnership between the new formal structure and the informal structure that will emerge? Explain.

2. Eventually, a great deal of participation in decisions will exist at every level of the organization.

    a. Is Bonnie being participative at the meeting?

    b. Why do you think she took the posture you have described?

3. Will the new jail have an extensive, moderate or lose formal structure? Explain.

4. Why did the Union president support her ideas?

Chapter 3
The Criminal Justice System in its Environment

Chapter Overview

In this chapter the interdependence of the criminal justice system and its environment is discussed. The focus is on the constraints environmental forces place on the system. These forces affect the mission of the system and its individual agencies as well as its objectives, policies, procedures, and day-to-day practices. In addition, how environmental forces allocate resources and personnel to the criminal justice system is discussed. Finally, environmental forces can be stable or complex and unpredictable; they often push the criminal justice system in contradictory directions. However, environmental forces will be the final determinants of the effectiveness and efficiency of that system. How environmental forces impose conflicting demands on members of criminal justice agencies and how those agencies attempt to survive in this complex environment is discussed.

An organization's environment is defined as any external phenomenon, event, group, individual, or system. This sweeping definition can be broken down into finite dimensions to make the concept of the interdependence of an organization and its environment understandable. The environment of an advanced society is composed of at least technological, legal, political, economic, demographic, ecological, and cultural forces (Hall, 1982). Each of these plays a role in creating, maintaining, changing, or purging organizations. As environmental conditions change, demands for goods and services, legal and resource limitations, and support for and opposition to the programs of both public and private organizations may also change. To adapt to new demands, constraints, and pressures, new bureaus or businesses may be created, and existing agencies alter their missions or policies. Agencies, public or private, that fail to meet changing demands, expectations, or constraints may suffer severe loss of resources or public support before they catch on. Those agencies that fail to catch on may become extinct. It is easy to understand how technological changes affect our lives as well as our organizations. Our ability to mass-produce electricity has improved our lives in general and made organizations increasingly productive. Yet the blessing has cursed us with acid rain and other pollution that may damage us severely in the not-to-distant future. To deal with the negative effects of pollution, the government, through new or existing agencies, has attempted to regulate the utility companies in response to public demands (political forces) for clean air and a safe environment. Every similar effort by government to regulate organizations or individuals will, in some manner, necessitate the use of agencies of the criminal justice system. Each of the environmental forces is discussed concerning the effect of each on the criminal justice system.

Learning Objectives

When finished studying this chapter the reader will be able to:

1. Discuss the major environmental influences of technology, law, economic conditions, demographic factors, cultural conditions, ecological conditions, and political conditions on the different agencies in the criminal justice systems.
2. Describe the political environment of the criminal justice system.
3. Define the major relationships between environmental uncertainty and decoupled organizations.
4. Discuss the most significant approach to managing environmental forces.
5. Define Influencing Input, Using Symbols, and Responding to Client Demand.

Key Terms

Environment
Civil Litigation
Economic Conditions
Cultural Conditions
Heterogeneous
Geographic Conditions
Political - Legal System
Simple Environment
Static Environment
Environmental Uncertainty
Service - Delivery
Dominant Coalition

Technology
Civil Rights Act
Demographic Factors
Homogeneous
Ecological Conditions
Political Conditions
Environmental States
Complex Environment
Dynamic Environment
Decoupled Organizations
Overlapping sub-groups
Work Processors

Chapter Outline

I. The Criminal Justice System in Its Environment
    A. The Environment is composed of Forces
        1. Technological
        2. Legal
        3. Political
        4. Economic

       5. Demographic
       6. Ecological
       7. Cultural
   B. As environmental conditions change public agencies must adapt.
       1. Forces affect agencies mission, policies and procedures.
       2. Agencies that fail to adapt lose resources or become extinct.

II. Defining the Environment of the Criminal Justice System
   A. Technology Changes
       1. Automobile has became a public safety problem.
       2. Community Policing has reduced use of patrol cars.
       3. Computers has allowed officers to communicate faster and from patrol cars.
       4. Video taping has reduced much guesswork.
       5. New high tech crimes now must be investigated.
   B. Law
       1. Criminal justice system is framed by legislation.
          a. Crimes and sentences are directed by legislation.
       2. Case Law
          a. Review of State and Federal court cases
          b. Civil litigation filed against criminal justice agencies.
          c. Cases with most effect are Federal cases.
       3. Civil Rights Act (1964)
          a. Criminal justice agencies have added women & minorities.
          b. Inmate civil suits have increased significantly.
   C. Economic Factors
       1. Agencies gain resources in good economic times
       2. Research on unemployment and crime rates is conflicting
          a. Increase of incarceration of African-American males is linked to economic conditions.
          b. Prison populations increase as unemployment increases.
          c. Income inequity is indicator of crime over poverty or unemployment.
   D. Demographic Factors
       1. Age, sex, race, ethnicity, and number of people in community have an impact on crime rates.
          a. Majority of criminal activity is done by people under age 25.
          b. Large cities have higher crime rates.
       2. Migration and immigration impact demographics and community organization.
          a. Immigrants converge in urban areas.
          b. Merging cultures manifest criminal behaviors.
   E. Cultural Conditions

1. Laws are codified social norms of a culture
   a. American culture is heterogeneous an dynamic.
   b. Public expectations of agencies conflict.
   c. We have a lack of consistency in norms and values.
2. Examples
   a. Prohibition
   b. War on Drugs

F. Ecological Conditions
   1. Geographical location-climate
   2. Size of Community - small communities tend to have homogeneous cultures.
   3. Economic base-industrial, service, agrarian

G. Political Conditions
   1. Governments react to changes in public opinions.
   2. Court decisions are made in certain political climates.
   3. Political pressure is directed by interest groups.
      a. MADD - DUI enforcement
      b. NAACP - fair treatment for black citizens
      c. Friends Service Committee -humane reform in prisons
      d. Police and Prison Officer Unions
   4. Cultural views and values become political.

III. The Political Environment of the Criminal Justice System
   A. Formal system includes legislating at federal, state, and local levels.
      1. These bodies pass legislation and allocate resources.
      2. They pass on demands of public to public service agencies.
      3. They are subjected to influence of pressure groups.
   B. Court System
      1. Judges make decisions congruent to their values.
      2. Judges reflect regional or political values.
   C. Informal Pressures
      1. Legislatures interfere with routine operations.
      2. Agencies respond directly to pressure from public.

IV. Task Environment Elements Specific to the Criminal Justice System
   A. Forces in the environment are directly related to agency goals.
      1. Beneficiaries
      2. Funders
      3. Providers of non-fiscal resource
      4. Providers of complementary services
      5. Competitors
      6. Legitamizers
   B. All elements are interdependent.

V. Environmental States
   A. Simple Environment
      1. External forces are homogeneous and few in number
      2. Example - police agencies in small communities
   B. Complex Environment
      1. External forces are heterogeneous and large in number
      2. Example - police agencies in large cities
   C. Static Environment
      1. Constant and stable over a period of time
      2. Jails with same number and type of inmates
   D. Dynamic Environment
      1. Unpredictable and changing over a period of time
      2. Urban police work

VI. Organizational Response to the Environment
   A. Environmental Uncertainty
      1. Dynamic and complex environments have greater uncertainty
         a. Lack of information relating to decision making
         b. Unknown cost of incorrect decisions
         c. Inability to estimate how probabilities will affect a decision
   B. Decoupled Organizations
      1. Large organizations tend to become decoupled.
      2. Environments may have two sub-environments.
         a. Political - legal (Dominant Coalition)
         b. Service - delivery (Work Processors)
      3. Overlapping sub-groups
         a. Dominant Coalition - small group of employees who oversee the organization and dictate policy decisions.
         b. Work Processors - majority of employees
         c. The cues, pressures and constraints sent to Dominant Coalition may differ from those faced by Work Processors.
C. The process of decentralizing, or federalizing, large bureaucracies is typically done so that the work process members have enough flexibility to deal with their local clientele or to respond to the demands of their local constituents. Decentralization is, in effect, a recognition that local environmental dimensions may be different at different levels of the organization and that the organization may face more than one environment.

VII. Managing Environmental Forces
   A. Organizations are open systems and are dependant on environmental systems for direction and resources.
      1. Criminal justice agencies get direction and resources from the political-legal and cultural systems.
   B. Influencing Input
      1. Legislators ask for input from agency heads.
      2. Agencies argue their positions based on their expertise.
      3. Agencies influence the open political system by gathering support from public groups.
      4. The news media act as a conduit between agencies and the environment.
   C. Using Symbols
      1. Goal statements of an agency making appear that the agency is conforming to the public's needs.
      2. Police "serve and protect", prison guards have become correction officers.
   D. Responding to Client Demand
      1. Agencies go beyond or ignore goals to meet clients needs.
      2. Police are granted much discretion to get the job done.
      3. Organizations try to control staff through procedures but it is difficult.
      4. Operational boundaries of criminal justice agencies are permeable.
   E. Decreasing Vulnerability to Pressure
      1. Agencies with limited resources and function in turbulent environments are forced to adapt or fail.
      2. Agencies must be open to interaction with the community

VIII. Implications for Administrators
   A. Administrator must protect the agency against improper environmental intrusions.
   B. Administrator must be in tune with the environment making and changes
      1. They should predict environmental changes and initiate planned change.
      2. They should resist idea that they work in a closed system.
      3. The administrator bears the responsibility for the agency's relationships with its environment.

Exercise

Students: Form into small groups (3-6 persons per group) and answer the questions following the case. Allow 20 to 25 minutes for preparation to report out findings. As the groups report consider discussions that relate to the chapter objectives, key words and the outline. The case is in the text in Chapter 3.

Case Study - Time To Dig Out

A confluence of forces and past decisions had placed the Governor and his party's legislatures in a difficult position. Major changes had to be made. The cost of the rapid prison construction of the last decade snuck up on the policy makers and was the central issue. Before the prison building binge, the department of corrections required only 1.7% of the total state budget. It increased to 15%, and is projected to rise substantially in the future. During that same time period, the industrial base of the state was changing from industry and production to service. Thus, the state's budget base was eroding concurrent with the dramatic increase in dollars allocated to prisons expansion. A budgetary consequence was that other state services were suffering from both the increased funding for corrections and the reduction in the states tax revenues. Supporters of higher education argued that state universities were under funded causing them to increase tuition to such a rate that a college education was to costly for working class families, who would, none the less, pay taxes that would fund higher education. In addition, funds for social welfare, mental health services, and state police were being limited. More importantly, perhaps, funds for parks, camp grounds and roads and highway construction was being rationed, threatening the states vibrant tourist business and a significant part of the state's tax base.

Recognizing this set of contingencies, the Governor, at the beginning of his second term said that there would be no further prison construction. Two new prisons were opened since to met the ever increasing influx of inmates. Citizens from an economically depressed region of the state are lobbying hard for a prison to be built in their area. Exacerbating the problem, the citizens voted overwhelmingly for a proposal sponsored by the governor to shift K - 12 school funding from property taxes by an increase in sales taxes by 2% and those funds would be disbursed by the state back to school districts. Supporters of K-12 education are still not satisfied with the level of funding and property owners are seeing attempts by local government to increase property taxes. Read the tax payers' lips "no more taxes."

The message is clear. The "carte blanch" funding for corrections is over. Moreover, legislators are finding it desirable to reduce funding for corrections in the not to distance future. However, legislators sense that the political climate is still in a frenzied anti-crime state driven by drive by shootings and other visible events even though the crime rate is not increasing and has cycled downward with the reduction of the size of the 15 to 25 year of age population. In fact, some legislators are discussing legislating a version of California "three strikes and out" criminal sentencing and others are attempting to outlaw radios and television set and other recreational opportunities for inmates to "get tough on crime."

The Governors response was to propose a "truth in sentencing" bill which would eliminate parole. This was sold as a get tougher on crime measure. However, some individuals close to the legislative process see "truth in sentencing" as an opportunity to review, change and control criminal sentencing to reduce the inmate population without reducing public safety while preserving a "tough on crime" posture. Recently, a conservative legislator announced an interest in changing legislation that guides criminal sentencing in the state. He is seeking guidance from the usual sources, judges, prosecuting attorneys, law enforcement and corrections officials. In addition, he will be consulting with criminal justice professors at universities across the state. No doubt, new legislation will appear in the state in the next few years and sentencing will be altered. How it will be altered, and how it will effect cost, public safety, the states budget and the political climate remains to be seen.

Case Study Questions

1. Identify the groups, organizations, political constituents, etc. that would support a reduction in funding for the department of corrections. Which of those groups would also publicly support changes in criminal sentencing that would reduce the prison population? Identify the stakeholders (groups or individuals who benefit) from the department of corrections or prison construction.

2. Identify the threats and opportunities to each component of the criminal justice system that are implicit in need to reverse expenditures for corrections to help "dig our way out" of the states fiscal problems.

3. What changes can the department of corrections anticipate in the near future? Spell out the best and worst case scenarios, keeping in mind when sentencing criminals is open for discussion and change, most legislators and a number of interest groups will throw their plans into the decision making hopper. How can the department of corrections effect the outcome?

Part II - The Individual in Criminal Justice Organizations

Chapter 4
Problems of Communication

Chapter Overview

The literature on both organizational theory and communication refers to communication as the "glue" that holds organizations together. Karl Weik (1979) describes the organizational process as a method to resolve ambiguities through the collectively processing of information. The typical organization-private firm, federal regulatory agency, police, court system or corrections agency is structured in some logical way. But whether the organization functions logically, in a coordinated manner, and achieves its goals depends greatly on the quality of its communication -- its ability to process information. Hence all members of an organization are given "permission," if not training, to communicate along certain pathways and within certain limits in order to facilitate coordination among members and among components of the organization. Most, if not all, organizational members understand the importance of communications. Poor communication, however, is often blamed for problems that occur within an organization. For example, when subordinates disobey directives and are difficult to control, it is often convenient for managers to assume communication is faulty rather than examine more fundamental issues such as the applicability of directives or the willingness of subordinates to follow orders. However, one may argue that distributing memoranda directing subordinates toward activities that are counter-productive is based upon a communication problem within the chain of command or hierarchy.

The pivotal question derived is what is meant by poor communication, or for that matter, communication. Communication impacts and is scripted by an organization's environmental forces, formal structure, human interactions of its members and clients, organizational politics and the theater in which organizational members play out their roles rich with symbols and self expression. Poor communication in the theater of human dialog in complex organizations implies meaning beyond a poorly worded memo or a broken FAX machine - although both phenomena contribute to poor communications. Identifying a break down in an organization as a function of faulty communication is often a convenient solvent for problems and is typically the tip of the proverbial iceberg. To understand communication in organizations - processing information through symbols and metaphors - it is important to understand the formal and informal pathways and hurdles through and over which information is determined to flow. The basic element of communication is a *dyad* two individuals transmitting symbols back and forth; or, more simply, two people communicating. The dyads may range from intimate to professional to ad hoc (Trenholm & Jensen, 1992). To understand the complexity of communication within organizations we can think of an infinite number of interchangeable *dyads* attempting to process information using an infinite number of symbols through a number of charted and uncharted pathways and over a number of identifiable and invisible hurdles.

This chapter is a attempt to briefly separate out and discuss the complexity of communication in the criminal justice system. The chapter begins with a description of the basic dyad and briefly discusses the hurdles and pathways faced by actors playing a role in the criminal justice system. We also apply the basic theories of communication to the individual practitioner in the criminal justice system, considering the unique and varied interactions practitioners have on a routine basis. We conclude with prescriptions for criminal justice administrators. The reader is admonished not to view communication as a phenomena separable from an organization's formal and informal structures and its culture. The communication *dyads* dance in a complex and changing community.

Learning Objectives

When finished studying this chapter the reader will be able to:
1. Discuss the four stages of the communication process.
2. Describe criminal justice examples of the eight barriers to communications.
3. Define non-verbal communication and communication load.
4. Discuss the most significant impact of the chain of command on effective communications.
5. Define Linking Pin Theory.

Key Terms

Encoding
Decoding
Preconceived Ideas
Use of Personalized Meanings
Non-Credibility of the Source
Poor Organizational Climate
Absolute Information
Communication with the Environment
Intra-Organizational Communication

Transmits
Barriers to Communication
Denial of Contrary Information
Lack of Motivation or Interest
Lack of Communication Skills
Use of Complex Channels
Distributed Information
Linking Pin

Chapter Outline

I. Basic Theory of Communication
    A. Process
        1. Encoding - sender determines to send the message.
        2. Transmits - sender conveys the message by a medium.
        3. Decoding - receiver interprets and determines meaning.
        4. Response - receiver responds back to sender (receiver).
    B. Barriers to Communication
        1. Preconceived ideas - receiver hears what he wants to hear.
        2. Denial of contrary information - if message conflicts with our personal beliefs or values, we may reject it or deny its validity (cognitive dissonance).
        3. Use of personalized meanings - words chosen by the sender may have different meaning to the receiver.
        4. Lack of motivation or interest - motivation in communicating and interest in the message must exist for both the sender and receiver.
        5. Non-credibility of the source - the sender may not be believable for several reasons and individuals with relatively greater status have more credibility than those with little status.
        6. Lack of communication skills - Poor communication skills can be attributed to an individual's lack of training, education level, experience, cognitive capacity, and personality traits.
        7. Poor organizational climate - very formal organizations may discourage all but formal and approved communications.
        8. Use of complex channels - the more gates communication must pass through the more likely the message will pass slowly and be altered.

II. Communication in Organizations
    A. Chain of Command
        1. Downward communication allows a clear path to send information to staff.
        2. Upward provides managers with a primary source of information.
        3. Horizontal communication facilitates coordination.
    B. Informal Communication
        1. Complex formal organizations breed the creation of the "grapevine."
        2. Informal gatekeepers filter information.
    C. Organizational Rules
        1. Flow of communications is dictated in policy and procedure.
        2. Rules include standard word usage procedural rules, methods of interactions.

D. Informal Communication Networks
   1. Communication between individuals within and between the official and informal subsystems.
   2. Exchange of new ideas is an innovation network
   3. "Kinship networks" are made up of members of a social group
E. Non-verbal Communication
   1. Symbols may stand on their own but they are usually integrated with verbal messages.
   2. Uniforms, guns, badges are non-verbal messages
   3. Individuals convey non-verbal messages through facial expressions, hand gestures, and other physical language.
F. Information and Communication
   1. Communication is the process of passing on information.
   2. Communication become the exchange of symbols that represent information.
G. Communication Load
   1. Load is the rate and complexity of communication inputs.
   2. Rate is the number of pieces on information that are received.
   3. Complexity is the number of judgements or factors involved.
   4. Three determinants of load
      a. Stable vs. unstable structure
      b. Capacity of individual or system to assimilate
      c. Individual's or system's desire to receive or send information
H. Absolute versus Distributed Information
   1. Absolute information is an idea or piece of knowledge expressed in recognized symbolic terms.
   2. Distributed information is an idea or piece of knowledge that is dispersed through a system.
I. Communication Roles for the Criminal Justice Practitioner
   1. Correction Officers
   2. Line Police Officers
   3. Prosecuting Attorneys
   4. Local Jail Administrators
J. Linking Pin
   1. Likert (1961) found that productivity in industry was highest in companies that were coordinated by a hierarchy of interlocking groups rather than by a traditional chain of command with its directed policies and procedures.
   2. The interlocking groups are bound together by linking pins, persons who serve as members of two or more groups or are part of the social system of two or more groups.
   3. Linking pins are individuals who make a concerted effort to have credibility and influence in their own units as well as in other

units that affect the efficient operation of their units.
4. The linking pin acts as an informal coordinator, making ad hoc efforts to smooth the work flow between units. The person acting as the linking pin could overcome the barriers of communication between units and probably establish an exchange system between units.

III. Implications for Criminal Justice Management
   A. Communication with the Environment
      1. The criminal justice system must provide society with a sense of personal and psychological safety.
      2. Administrators need to develop routinized methods of providing useful information to the public and political systems.
      3. There is a deep distrust between criminal justice and media.
      4. Victims who are kept advised of case progress are typically satisfied.
   B. Intra Organizational Communications
      1. Intra Organizational relationships and communication within the system are, by design, ineffective.
      2. High quantity and quality of contact between staff of agencies decreases conflict.
   C. General Considerations
      1. There is a link between effective communications and efficiency in human services.
      2. Agencies should teach values, priorities, and language of groups they regularly deal with to their organizational members.
      3. Agencies can improve interagency communication by informing members about conflict issues.
      4. Large organizations should seek to promote and control lateral communication within and between agencies.

Exercise

Students:

Give a specific example of a criminal justice organizational <u>situation</u> for each of the following barriers to communication;

1. Preconceived Ideas

2. Denial of Contrary Information

3. Use of Personalized Meanings

4. Lack of Motivation or Interest

5. Non credibility of the Source

6. Lack of Communications Skills

7. Poor Organization Climate

8. Use of Complex Channels

Chapter 5
Motivation of Personnel

Chapter Overview

Motivation can be viewed in two ways. First, one can view motivation as a psychological concept, examining the state of mind of the individual and why he or she exhibits a certain type of behavior. For example, it has been said that American culture values the work ethic. Much of this attitude can be traced to personal values that are transmitted to children in their formative years. Learned values, therefore, play a critical role in whether a person is motivated to perform various tasks. (later in this chapter we will discuss those factors that lead or cause one to act in a certain fashion, from both a human and an organizational point of view.) The psychological definition of motivation depends on how the individual perceives the world and on the "psychological contract" between the individual and the work environment (Schein, 1970). With respect to criminal justice, one could ask, for example, what factors motivate people to become police officers, or, more importantly, what factors in the police environment motivate individuals to do their jobs? Even more telling would be an examination of those structures in the police organization that promote the fulfillment of individual needs while at the same time motivating people to do their jobs.

Second, motivation can be examined from an organizational point of view, exploring the kinds of managerial behavior that induce employees to act in a way consistent with the expectations and demands of the organization. This organizational way of examining motivation enables one to explore motivational strategies that promote the best interests of both the individual and the organization. A sense of congruence between the employee and the organization is sought, and the responsibility of management is to provide mechanisms that enable employees to be highly motivated and moved to do the work expected of them. In criminal justice agencies, one could ask, for example, how the administrator of a police organization or a correctional institution motivates employees or what the best strategies for motivating rank-and-file police officers or corrections officers are.

In the remainder of this chapter, we attempt to provide answers to these questions. Our discussion focuses on those theories of motivation that have guided criminal justice research. Because there has not been much research on motivation in the criminal justice system, we review pertinent theories and studies that address issues fundamental to criminal justice. In addition, we provide some prescriptions for criminal justice systems based on our understanding of motivation. To begin, we examine several different theories of motivation.

Learning Objectives

When finished studying this chapter the reader will be able to:

1. List and briefly discuss the six theories of motivation of personnel.
2. Describe needs theory and relate it to a criminal justice personnel scenario.
3. Define quality circle programs.
4. Define management by objectives.
5. List and briefly discuss the six elements of developing an integrated model of motivation.

Key Terms

Maslow
Theory X and Theory Y
Achievement-Power Theory
Expectancy Theory
Theory Z
Management by Objectives

Need theory
McGregor
McClelland
Equity Theory
Quality circles

Chapter Outline

I. Theories of Motivational of Personnel
    A. Need theory
        1. The most recognized theory of motivation comes from the work of Maslow (1943). He argued that one can examine motivation as one result of various physical and psychological needs. The central theme of need theory is that all people have needs, both physical and psychological, which affect their behavior patterns. Maslow argued that human beings have five basic needs.
            a. *Physiological needs* assure the basic survival of the individual. Included in this need category are food and water. Physical well-being must be assured before any other needs can be fulfilled.
            b. *Safety and security.* Human beings require that they be safe in their environments and free from any threat of attack by aggressors. In addition, people need to know that there is a secure and certain environment in which they can act as social beings.

c. *Belonging needs* are reflected in the desire to be loved and to belong to a group. In addition, people need to have and show affection toward other human beings. This need may be expressed either in joining groups or by receiving support from one's family, friends, and relatives.

d. *Self esteem - one's self-image and how one is viewed by peers.* Individuals seek prestige and recognition from their loved ones and their fellow workers. Self confidence is intricately tied to this perception of self worth.

e. *Self actualization* needs center around one's potential to grow and to do one's best in endeavors. According to Maslow, these needs are different for every individual, which is why it is difficult to develop a motivational strategy that is able to meet the self-actualization needs of all employees.

2. The hierarchy is divided into higher-order needs and primary needs.

   a. higher-order needs are belonging, esteem, and self-actualization.

   b. primary needs are physiological and for safety and security.

B. Theory X and Theory Y

1. The second theory of motivation is composed of two parts: Theory X and Theory Y and is based on the work of McGregor (1978). In his seminal article entitled "The Human Side of Enterprise," McGregor describes these two approaches to human behavior and management. These approaches are based on a number of assumptions about human behavior.

2. Theory X is derived from three fundamental beliefs; McGregor (1978) considers these beliefs the conventional view of management.

   a. Management is responsible for organizing the elements of productive enterprise-money, materials, equipment, people-for economic ends.

   b. With respect to people, management directs their efforts, motivates them, controls their actions, and modifies their behavior to fit the needs of the organization.

   c. Without active intervention by management, people would ignore-even resist-organizational needs. They must therefore be persuaded, rewarded, punished, controlled; their activities must be directed.

3. Theory Y, which views the human condition in an optimistic way, is based on the following assumptions:

   a. Management is responsible for organizing the elements of

productive enterprise-money, materials, equipment, people-for economic ends.
  b. People are not ignorant of or resistant to organizational needs. They have become so as a result of their experience in organizations.
  c. Motivation, potential for development, capacity for assuming responsibility, and readiness to direct behavior toward organizational goals are present in people. Management does not put them there. It is a responsibility of management to make it possible for people to recognize and develop these attributes themselves.
  d. The essential task of management is to arrange organizational conditions and methods of operation so that people can achieve their own goals by directing their own efforts toward organizational objectives.
C. Achievement-Power Theory
  1. The achievement theory of motivation was originally developed by McClelland (1968). In addition, attention is now being paid to the power motive. It seems appropriate to discuss these two motives (achievement and power) together.
  2. Achievement - Individuals can be led toward specific behaviors because these behaviors produce feelings of achievement. People with high achievement values do the following:
    a. Seek to achieve success through their own efforts and not have their success attributed to other factors.
    b. Work on projects that are challenging but not impossible.
    c. Receive identifiable and recurring feedback about their work and avoid situations where their level of achievement is in question.
  3. Power Motive - A growing body of literature attempts to document the role that power plays in organizations, particularly in decision-making processes The power motive can be defined as a person's need to have some type of influence over another's behavior.
    a. Personalized Power, as manifested through an adversarial relationship; person-to-person competition is emphasized, and domination is a by-product. People are viewed simplistically as winners and losers, with the main goal being the achievement of power over others.
    b. Socialized Power is impersonal and is expressed through a concern for others; it is employed by individuals who are sensitive to the fact that someone's gain means another

person's loss. This type of power orientation is humanistic and is employed by those in leadership roles in social organizations

D. Expectancy Theory
   1. Expectancy theory is based on the belief that if a certain amount of effort is put forth, a calculated outcome will result.
   2. It is a rational approach to motivation.
   3. Valences are the level of satisfaction or dissatisfaction produced by various outcomes.
   4. Example - police officers motivational levels are a function of what they expect and what valence they assign to their various activities.
   5. If employee is constantly rewarded, both intrinsinctly and extrinsinctly, he or she should be satisfied.

E. Equity Theory
   1. Equity theory holds that an individual's motivation level is affected by his/her perception of fairness in the workplace. The theory holds that individual motivation must be understood in relation to how other employees are treated by management and the organization. Fundamentally, equity theory stresses the importance of fairness in the organization and how employees perceive its application in the work force.
   2. Equity theory postulates two fundamental assumptions:
      a. individuals evaluate their interpersonal relationships as they would any other commodity.
      b. individuals develop expectations concerning their evaluation in the organization equivalent to the amount of individual contribution they make.
   3. Equity theory is based on inputs and outputs as perceived by the employee.
      a. Inputs examples are age, seniority, training and education.
      b. Outputs examples are promotion, salary, recognition, and benefits.

F. Theory Z
   1. Theory Z is viewed as a holistic approach to management and administration. With respect to employee motivation, Theory Z recommends broad changes and reforms.
   2. Theory Z is based on three beliefs:
      a. There is among management a concern for production, a position expressed in Theory X.
      b. There is among management a concern for the well-being of workers as productive employees. This position is similar to a basic assumption of Theory Y.

c. Finally, and the belief that distinguishes Theory Z from Theory X and Y, the organization cannot be viewed independently of the larger social, economic, and political conditions in society.
3. Archambeault and Wierman (1983 suggest several changes that have to occur in the management of police organizations in order for police to become more responsive than they now are to their employees and their communities.
   a. There must be shared decision making in police organizations, with individual officers having increased input on matters that affect them, although management would still be the final authority on key administrative issues.
   b. Supporters of Theory Z suggest that there be a team approach to policing, with the emphasis on the collective responsibility of officers. The idea here would be to get police away from the traditional notion of individual responsibility and individual work.
   c. Police officers would have a clearly identified career path, with attendant rewards and promotional opportunities laid out in advance.
   d. Police organizations must be more "holistic" in its dealings with police officers by appreciating the fact that officers exist in society. They have needs beyond the work setting, including, educational, personal, and family needs.

II. Prescriptions for Criminal Justice Management
   A. One key element links all these differing approaches to employee motivation: the needs, perspectives, and viewpoints of employees are instrumental not only to their individual growth but also to organizational effectiveness.
      1. More directly, it would be accurate to conclude that effective criminal justice management recognizes that the motivation of employees requires the growth and maturity of those employees through proactive and flexible management strategies.
      2. The present challenge to police managers is to provide a work climate in which every employee has the opportunity to mature, both as an individual and as a member of the department. However, the police manager must believe that individuals can be essentially self-directed and creative in their work environments if they are motivated by the management.

B. While cognizant of the fact that the management of criminal justice systems is different from the management of private companies or other public institutions, a number of programs can be taken from these other sectors and applied effectively to criminal justice processes. Two of these programs are: quality circles and Management by Objectives.
   1. Quality Circle Programs - Quality circle programs are based on two fundamental assumptions.
      a. Interactions among employees should provide for the maximum growth of the individual. Quality circles are meant to enhance the ability of workers to improve themselves, both personally and professionally.
      b. By providing conditions for the growth of employees, the organization will become increasingly effective. In short, it is in the best interests of the organization to promote the well-being of workers.
      c. Operating on these two assumptions, quality circle programs are defined as small groups of employees, typically non-management personnel from the same work unit, who meet regularly to identify, analyze, and select solutions to problems relating to the work unit.
      d. Within the police subsystem of the criminal justice process, researchers have strongly recommended this approach. Hatry and Greiner (1984) suggest that the use of quality circle programs greatly enhances the potential for producing small-scale service improvements and improving work-unit morale among officers. These improvements are crucial, in our opinion, to the motivation of police officers.
      e. This approach to improving the motivational levels of police officers is also applicable to other workers in the criminal justice process, e.g., corrections officers, counselors, and court personnel.
C. Management by Objectives (MBO)
   1. MBO can be defined as a process whereby individual managers and employees identify goals and work toward their completion and evaluation within a specific time period.
      a. A lack of commitment only breeds contempt for and disapproval of the program in lower-level employees.
      b. Administrative staff must be able to receive criticism and suggestions from employees. Otherwise, management will not be attuned to the workings of the organization.
      c. Any MBO program must take into consideration the power

structure in the organization. It is often difficult for managers to share power with subordinates.

d. Workers as well as management must believe that the MBO process is worth pursuing. In many organizations, lack of commitment has led to the demise of MBO programs.

D. An Integrated Model of Motivation

1. An example of an integrated model of motivation that may be useful to criminal justice employees (California Department of Corrections, 1994). This model would be based on key elements of the theories and literature discussed above. The model has six basic elements:

   a. Personal Motives and Values are Important. Criminal justice workers have motives and values that stress public service as well as personal interests in having a profession that is appreciated and remunerated fairly and appropriately.

   b. Use of Incentives and Rewards. Employees must be rewarded for good work. The types of rewards can be varied.

   c. Reinforcement. Administrators must develop feedback mechanisms such that workers understand that their performance is appropriate given assigned tasks.

   d. Specific and Clear Goals. All theories of motivation highlight the importance of goals or expected outcomes to the motivation process.

   e. Personal and Material Resources. The organization must have a sufficient number of resources, both human and financial, that create a motivating environment for employees.

   f. Interpersonal and Group Processes Must Support Members' Goals. In criminal justice organizations, this means the development of work groups that identify with employees' individual interests, as well as groups concerns.

2. The goal is to create a motivational environment such that maximum effort can be exhibited by employees.

Exercise

Analyze the following case in relation to each of the six motivational theories. Report out on the effects of the actions in the case on Loretta and on the other members of the organization.

Ensure that you consider all of the six theories:
>Need theory
>
>Theory X and Theory Y
>
>Achievement-Power Theory
>
>Expectancy Theory
>
>Equity Theory
>
>Theory Z.

Case Study - Loretta and Butch

Loretta was a social worker in the Outofit County Jail in Wolfpoint, Montana. The sheriff, Butch Nobrainer, had just received a conditions of confinement lawsuit concerning the jail operation and physical plant. He was advised by the county attorney that he and the county were in serious trouble. The county attorney recommended that the jail be changed immediately starting with the appointment of a professional jail administrator.

The sheriff appointed Loretta at the recommendation of the district judge. The judge had reported that loretta was the only person working in the jail that was smart enough to know what to do. Loretta quickly went to work compiling a list of potential important changes. She was very enthusiastic, working 16 hour days interviewing all employees, working with line level workers and meeting regularly with supervisors. She created teams of officers for the purpose of identifying strategies for solving problems. She designed an organizational structure that encouraged feedback from line level officers.

The teams were assigned to develop a realistic policy and procedures manual that reflected constitutional requirements for jail operation. They were to identify goals and objectives of the organization and to identify the critical tasks officers in which should be trained. Loretta had developed the plan for change and had started the process for writing new policies. She was working harder than she had ever worked in her life but she was very happy. She had seen the problems develop in the jail but had been helpless to do anything about them because her role was limited to helping inmate solve family and other social problems. Now she was making important decisions, learning important managerial skills and creating important changes that would benefit the department and the county.

Loretta approached the sheriff with her organizational change plan and requested (1) authorization to implement the plan fully; (2) an increase in budget for overtime and officer training and (3) weekly meetings with the sheriff for the purpose of communicating progress and discussing problems. In response, Butch informed Loretta that she was not to make any decisions of any kind without his approval He stated that she was allowing too much officer freedom which was contrary to the organization's philosophy He stated that there was no need for a policies and procedures manual and that he did not have the time to meet with her weekly.

Loretta found that her proposed changes could not be made under the sheriff's restrictions and she soon quit the position. She transferred to a county job service position counseling the unemployed. The sheriff's department was taken to federal court for failing to meet the legal requirements and they were forced through a consent decree to make the necessary changes in the jail operations. The county was sued for 3 million dollars and the sheriff paid $50,000 from his personal funds.

Chapter 6
Job Design

Chapter Overview

In criminal justice the design of jobs is often taken for granted: police officers police, corrections officers guard, probation officers manage their caseloads, and judges deliberate. It is often assumed that these tasks govern the design of work. Both theory and research in industrial settings question such assumptions. The term job design has been used to describe the "deliberate, purposeful planning of the job including all of its structural and social aspects and their effect on the employee"

Top administrators can no longer, if they ever could, bring about major changes in operating philosophy through fiat. And serious limits exist on what can be achieved simply by reassigning personnel, changing the organizational structure, recruiting new personnel, and conducting training programs. Problem-oriented policing, with its strong commitment to engaging rank-and-file officers more fully in the operation of the police agency, greatly increases the likelihood that rank-and-file officers will support needed change, because they are an essential part of t. We are at work for much of our lives. For many of us, also, work is not only a place where tasks are accomplished but an experience that adds to the value and meaning of our lives. Although we have many work-related personal goals, our jobs fulfill organizational goals. Our efforts may contribute to the control of crime, the processing of offenders, or the treatment of those convicted.

This chapter examines the interplay of these personal and organizational goals. This chapter focuses on how the structure of work can satisfy or fail to satisfy these goals. Also examined are some of the undesirable consequences of poorly designed work.

Learning Objectives

When finished studying this chapter the reader will be able to:

1. List and briefly discuss the six "psychological job requirements".

2. List and briefly discuss the significant job characteristics for employee motivation.

3. Define vertical and horizontal job enrichment.

4. Relate management by objectives to job design.

Key Terms

Job Design
Personal Growth
Task Identity
Autonomy

Psychological Job Requirements
Skill Variety
Task Significance
Feedback

Chapter Outline

I. There are many approaches to job design and many lists of criteria for a good job. Although efficiency was once the chief concern, a wide variety of other goals have been recognized. One popular list of "psychological job requirements" includes the following factors (Emmery and Emmery, 1974)

    A. Adequate elbowroom - Workers need a sense that they are their own bosses and that accept in unusual circumstances they will not have a boss breathing down their necks. But they don't want so much elbowroom that they don't know what to do next.

    B. Chances to learn on the job and go on learning - Such learning is possible only when people are able to set goals that are reasonable challenges for them and to know results in time for them to correct their behavior.

    C. An optimal level of variety - Workers need to be able to vary the work, so as to avoid boredom and fatigue and to gain the best advantage from settling into a satisfying rhythm of work.

    D. Help and respect from work mates - Workers need to avoid conditions where it is in no one's interest to lift a finger to help another, where people are pitted against each other so that one persons gain is another's loss, and where the individual's capabilities or inabilities are denied.

    E. A sense that one's work meaningfully contributes to social welfare - Workers do not want a job that could be done well by a trained monkey or an industrial robot machine. They also do not want to feel that society would probably be better served by not having the job done, or at least not having it done so shoddily.

    F. A desirable future - Workers do not want dead-end jobs; they want ones get continue to allow personal growth.

II. Significant Job Characteristics for Employee Motivation
- A. Skill Variety - the degree to which jobs require a variety of different activities, skills, and talents.
- B. Task Identity - the degree to which a job requires the completion of a whole, task rather than bits or pieces of a project.
- C. Task Significance - the extent to which a job has a meaningful impact on others; the importance of the job.
- D. Autonomy - the degree of freedom, independence, and discretion provided by a job.
- E. Feedback - the extent to which workers get direct and clear information.

III. Job Redesign in Criminal Justice and Other Human Services
- A. Human services workers often value the most enriched aspects of their work or even take steps to enrich their own jobs.
- B. Toch (1978) found that 20 percent of a sample of corrections officers were independently experimenting with nontraditional enriched roles.
- C. Enrichment (vertical loading) is redesigning the job to be more rewarding.
- D. Enlargement (horizontal loading) is redesigning the job to include a variety of duties.

Exercise

Students: Consider discussions that relate to the chapter objectives, key words and the outline.

In 1975, the Boulder, Colorado Sheriff's Department changed the titles of its jail officers to corrections specialists. The department instituted an operational idea labeled the "two hat" approach. This approach required that officers be responsible for both custody and treatment. They were trained in individual and group counseling skills and, at the same time, they were trained in self defense and firearms skills. The officers participated in an MBO program that required setting objectives and determining evaluation criteria for their work areas. The officers were required to learn all of the different jobs in the jail division and they were considered to be generalists rather than being allowed to specialize in one specific job.

1. What theoretical approaches were the basis this job redesign project?

2. What problems, if any, do you envision in the long run with the Boulder model?

3. How would you redesign the jail officer job to create more sources of motivation and eliminate characteristics of dissatisfaction or burnout?

Chapter 7
Leadership

Chapter Overview

Many interested in the administration of criminal justice today have addressed the issue of leadership. The contemporary criminal justice administrator is expected to be an effective leader, an expectation that fits with the general demand for competent leaders in all organizations, both public and private. Although a great deal of prescriptive material describes for the criminal justice administrator how to lead an organization effectively, little empirical evidence shows what effective leadership entails. More importantly, few of the existing theoretical models of leadership created in other disciplines, which may be useful to the criminal justice administrator, have been applied to this area.

In this chapter, a review of the relevant aspects of leadership and apply our understanding of the leadership process to the components of the criminal justice system is provided. The review, however, is not prescriptive. Instead, we offer an analytical framework for understanding the process of leadership in criminal justice organizations. This framework is rooted in empirical research and theoretical models of leadership. In this way, we hope not only to provide increased understanding of this process but in addition to suggest what can and cannot be expected from criminal justice leaders. To accomplish these objectives, several areas are explored. First, we define leadership and argue that because criminal justice administration is fundamentally politically driven, it is useful to understand leadership within the political arena.

Second, the chapter reviews the major theories of leadership that have been developed in research on organizational behavior. Our discussion in this section integrates what we know about leadership research done in other organizations and applies these findings to the criminal justice system. Our review in this section includes an analysis of both behavioral and contingency theories of leadership. Both show promise for explaining the leadership process in criminal justice.

Finally, the chapter explores the criminal justice research that addresses the issue of leadership. Although much of this literature is overly prescriptive and does not reflect the realities of criminal justice organizations, we provide an overview of those few pieces of research that empirically test theoretical models of leadership. We then make some recommendations for future research on leadership in criminal justice organizations. In addition, we will be presenting a model of leadership education that has been operationalized within a department of corrections.

Learning Objectives

When finished studying this chapter the reader will be able to:

1. Define four major elements of leadership.
2. Discuss the eleven techniques of leadership influence.
3. Define the two behavioral models of leadership.
4. Define the " Management Grid".
5. Define the Ohio State and Michigan theories of leadership.
6. Define the Contingency theories.

Key Terms

Situational Leadership
Behavioral Models
Fiedler's Contingency Theory
Ohio State Theory
Michigan Theory
Path-Goal Theory

Management Grid
Authoritarian
Directive Leadership
Supportive Leadership
Achievement-Oriented
Participative Leadership

Chapter Outline

I. Leadership Defined
    A. Four distinct, yet not separate, ideas about administration guide our definitions of leadership.
        1. First, leadership is a process that effectively accomplishes organizational goals. One cannot conceptually separate leadership from organizational effectiveness (Tosi, Rizzo, and Carroll, 1986), from the accomplishment of objectives.
        2. Second, leadership can be learned by people in administrative positions in organizations.
            a. Much of the literature in criminal justice management assumes that effective leadership can be taught.
        3. Third, the leadership process is a group process.
            a. To accomplish organizational objectives, leaders must influence a number of people.
            b. The process of leadership must thus be examined in light of how leaders get people to achieve the tasks necessary for organizational existence and survival.
        4. Fourth, leadership in public bureaucracies like the agencies of

criminal justice is inherently political and must be examined within the political arena.
- a. Leadership in organizations is often discussed with an internal focus.
- b. Little is said about the external nature of leadership, even though an external view is critical to a complete understanding of how public agencies are run.

B. Yukl (1981) suggests eleven different techniques of influence that affect the leadership process:

1. *Legitimate request.* A person complies with an agent's request because the person recognizes the agent's "right" to make such a request.
2. *Instrumental compliance.* A person is induced to alter his or her behavior by an agent's implicit or explicit promise to ensure some tangible outcome desired by the person.
3. *Coercion.* A person is induced to comply by an agent's explicit or implicit threat to ensure adverse outcomes if the person fails to do so.
4. *Rational persuasion.* A person is convinced by an agent that the suggested behavior is the best way for the person to satisfy his or her needs or to attain his or her objectives.
5. *Rational faith.* An agent's suggestion is sufficient to evoke compliance by a person without the necessity for any explanation.
6. *Inspirational appeal.* A person is persuaded by an agent that there is a necessary link between the requested behavior and some value that is important enough to justify the behavior.
7. *Indoctrination.* A person acts because of induced internalization of strong values that are relevant to the desired behavior.
8. *Information distortion.* A person is influenced, without being aware of it, by an agent's limiting, falsifying, or interpreting information in a way that is conducive to compliance.
9. *Situational engineering.* A person's attitudes and behavior are indirectly influenced by an agent's manipulation of relevant aspects of the physical and social situation.
10. *Personal identification.* A person imitates an agent's attitudes and behavior because the person admires or worships the agent.
11. *Decision identification.* An agent allows a person to participate in and have substantial influence over the making of a decision, thereby gaining the person's identification with the final choice.

C. Leader uses to any one or a combination of these techniques can be used. Regardless of method, however, effective leaders are able to get subordinates to work toward the stated objectives of the

organization.
   1. These techniques are different from styles of leadership.
   2. A style of leadership consists of all the techniques to achieve organizational goals.

D. Leadership in criminal justice agencies involves convincing both subordinates and those outside in the political arena that a particular method (usually the leader's) is the best one for accomplishing organizational objectives.

E. Leadership is tied to the effectiveness of an organization; as being able to be learned depending on the tasks, functions, and objectives of the organization; as being carried out in a group setting; and, probably most importantly in criminal justice agencies, as having political and public foci.

II. Theories of Leadership

A. The first approach, and probably the oldest, is based on the instincts of the leader.
   1. It is assumed that a leader is born and not made. This approach tends to emphasize inherent personality traits of the individual.
   2. In addition, it assumes that leadership can be evaluated on the basis of the personality characteristics of the leader.
   3. It is difficult to know whether the leader's personality makeup is critical to the leadership process or whether particular traits of a leader are required for a goal to be achieved.
   4. Because of a number of difficulties associated with this approach, it has been largely abandoned by those interested in studying the leadership process.

B. The behavioral approach emphasizes the behaviors of individual leaders.
   1. Behavioral approaches fall into two distinct areas:
      a. The distribution of influence and
      b. The task and social behaviors of leaders.

C. The final approach to examining the phenomenon of leadership is referred to as the contingency method.
   1. This approach is relatively recent and tends to emphasize multiple variables, particularly situational variables that constrain leadership.
      a. These situational variables include:
         (1) characteristics of subordinates,
         (2) the organizational context,
         (3) the style of leadership.

III. Behavioral Models
  A. This approach suggests that effective leadership depends on how the leader behaves and acts with subordinates.
    1. The behavioral approach accentuates how leaders initiate interactions with subordinates to get them to accomplish organizational tasks.
    2. This process is known as initiating structures.
  B. Behavioral approaches are concerned with how the employee is able to achieve personal goals within the organization while simultaneously accomplishing the central tasks of the organization.
  C. They evolved from two separate sets of leadership studies done in the 1940s, 1950s, and early 1960s:
    1. The Ohio State Studies and
    2. The Michigan Studies.
  D. A popular model of supervision was created at this time; it is known as the managerial grid.
    1. Originally devised by Blake and Mouton (1964), this grid was based on two dimensions of behavior-"concern for people" and "concern for production."
    2. These dimensions are similar to the concepts of consideration and initiating structure.
    3. The most effective manager is one who is both concerned with high levels of production among employees and sensitive to their needs. There has been considerable application of the managerial grid to criminal justice (see Duffee, 1986).
  E. The Ohio State Studies states that leadership could be examined on the two dimensions of consideration and initiating structure.
    1. Consideration is the leader's expression of concern for subordinates' feelings, ideas, and opinions about job-related matters.
      a. Considerate leaders are concerned about employees, develop trust between themselves and subordinates, and more often than not develop good communication between themselves and workers.
    2. Initiating structure is the leader's direction of himself or herself and of subordinates toward specific goals.
      a. The role of the leader is to make sure that an adequate structure is available for employees so that organizational objectives are accomplished.
    3. The Ohio State Studies concluded that effective leadership is present in an organization when the levels of consideration and initiating structure are high among leaders.
      a. The production-centered supervisor and the

employee-centered supervisor.
4. According to the Michigan Studies, the effective leader, on the whole, attempts to be employee centered, which in turn engenders productive subordinates. It is questionable whether the phenomenon of leadership can be understood as being either employee centered or production centered.
5. It is not clear that either the Ohio State Studies or the Michigan

IV. Contingency Theories
   A. Contingency theories of leadership differ from both trait and behavioral theories in that they emphasize the situation or context.
      1. Fiedler's contingency model and the path-goal theory.
      2. Each has distinctive elements that contribute to our understanding of leadership in criminal justice organizations.
      3. In addition, from each model we can draw different implications for the management and administration of the systems of criminal justice.
   B. Fiedler's Contingency Model
      1. According to Fiedler (1967), the leadership process is constrained by three major situational dimensions.
      2. First, leader-member relations are the level of trust and the degree of likeness that the leader has with subordinate groups.
         a. The leader who is not liked or well received by subordinates is constrained by this situation and can be ineffective in guiding and influencing workers to accomplish organizational tasks.
      3. Second, the task structure of the organization is, in Fiedler's (1967) words, "the degree to which the task is spelled out ... or must be left nebulous and undefined".
         a. Routinized task structure has clearly defined procedures for accomplishing organizational objectives.
         b. It is easier to lead when the task structure is clearly defined and open to direct monitoring by the supervisor.
         c. The organization with an undefined task structure or uncertainty as to how a certain objective is to be achieved presents problems.
      4. Third, the position power of the leader is the ability of the leader to exercise power in the organization. Fiedler's test of position power is the ability to hire and fire subordinates.
         a. A leader with high position power is able to hire or fire at will. A leader with low position power has limited authority to dismiss someone or bring an individual into

the organization.
C. Given these situational dimensions-leader-member relations, task structure, and position power-we can match the proper leadership styles with the right situations to produce the most effective form of leadership.
   1. Fiedler suggests that task-production leaders tend to be more effective in structured situations, while human relations-oriented leaders are more effective in situations that require a creative response on the part of supervisors and subordinates.
D. In addition, high situational control exists for a leader when there are good leader-member relations, a high task structure, and the leader has high position power.
   1. Low situational control exists when the opposite conditions are present: poor leader-member relations, low task structure, and the leader has little or no position power.
   2. Moderate situation control means the situational characteristics are mixed. Some characteristics work to the advantage of the leader (for example, high leader-member relations) while others do not.
E. The human relations-oriented leader will be the most successful where the group has structured tasks and a dislike for the leader. Additionally, the human relations-oriented leader is effective in a situation where the group likes the leader and has an unstructured task.
F. Two basic criticisms can be leveled against this theory of leadership.
   1. First, Fiedler implys that leaders are either task oriented or human relations oriented. The theory does not admit the possibility that leaders could be equally high on both dimensions.
   2. Second, there is an implicit assumption in this theory that task structure and leader-member relations cannot be modified or changed by the leader's style.
G. Path-goal theory
   1. path-goal theory suggests that the interaction between leader behavior and the situational aspects of the organization is important (House and Mitchell, 1985).
   2. This theory argues that leadership is linked to an expectancy theory of motivation (see chapter 4), which posits that the leader's behavior has a direct impact on the actions of employees if it is a source of satisfaction for them.
   3. Leader behavior is viewed as effective if the leader is able to make satisfaction for employees contingent on good or positive performance.
H. Effective leadership is tied to the degree of direction and guidance that

the leader can provide in the work situation. This guidance and direction can be tied to four styles of leadership.
1. Directive leadership emphasizes the expectations of the leader and the tasks to be performed by subordinates.
    a. The leader instills into subordinates the importance of the rules and regulations of the organization and their relationship to task performance.
    b. The leader provides the necessary guidance to subordinates to motivate them to accomplish the tasks required by the organization.
2. Supportive leadership stresses a concern for employees.
    a. This type of leader is friendly with employees and desires to be approachable. The primary concern of the leader is both to accomplish the tasks of the organization and to meet the needs of the workers.
3. Participative leadership emphasizes collaboration of the leader and subordinates.
    a. The leader employing this style attempts to involve subordinates in the decision-making process of the organization and to assure them of their importance in the organization.
4. Achievement-oriented leadership is concerned with having subordinates produce results.
    a. This leader expects that workers will attempt to do their best, and that if goals are set high enough and subordinates are properly motivated, they will achieve those goals.
    b. The leader thus has confidence that employees will achieve the stated goals and tasks.

Exercise

Students: In your small groups answer the issues concerning the case. Consider the chapter objectives, key words and the outline.

Apply the leadership theories to the case and to focus on what Clark did wrong and what should he have done to resolve the issues.

Case Study - Dogpatch County

Sheriff Dick Clark was recently elected to office primarily in response to a demand from the public to reorganize and "fix" the corrupt Dogpatch County Sheriff's Department. Dick, a local city police officer who had been named officer of the month several times for his outstanding "street policing" record, moved quickly after taking office. He immediately announced, first, that all Dogpatch Sheriff's Department employees would be required to reapply for their jobs if they wanted to work for him (eventually hired 18 of the 75 persons applying) and, second, he named his old car partner, Ralph Sandoval, as Undersheriff and 4 other policemen and detectives as captains. All of the top six managers, the sheriff, Undersheriff and four captains, had been looking for promotions or new jobs and this opportunity to take over the Sheriff's Department was important to all of them.

Clark and Sandoval became a quick moving team that made many changes and directed everyone in the organization with an "iron hand". They held daily 7:30AM meetings with the captains at which they gave orders to the captains relating to the changes they wanted to make. These changes or orders included issues as how to perform major investigations, how to reorganize the records system, which personnel to hire or fire or promote and which areas required proactive patrolling.

After three months, the captains, at a morning meeting, declared that there were many problems with the management process. They stated that:
(1) they needed more freedom in running their divisions,
(2) they needed time to talk and solve problems laterally with each other,
(3) they did not feel effective or influential with their staffs,
(4) there was a high turnover rate already and it was hard to get out of a crisis management mode of doing things and
(5) they were all frustrated with their jobs and did not see a difference with where they were in the police department.

In response, Clark and Sandoval, after meeting alone for three days, presented a reorganization plan for the department that placed Sandoval in a position of having more direct control over the day to day law enforcement functions and jail and Clark direct control over the day to day support and civil functions. After three more months, the four captains all turned in resignations and the department's turnover rate continued to increase.

Chapter 8
Personnel Supervision and Evaluation

Chapter Overview

Previous chapters have examined the importance of motivation, job design, and leadership to criminal justice administration. These issues are central to the smooth functioning of criminal justice organizations, yet another critical issue facing criminal justice administrators is personnel supervision and evaluation. Chapter two described the nature and structure of criminal justice organizations, but what was not examined was how within the structures of criminal justice organizations employees are actually supervised and evaluated. This chapter will examine the topic of supervision and evaluation as it relates to individual performance. Appropriate models of employee supervision will be explored within the context of an organizational setting. The issue of organizational effectiveness will not be addressed in this chapter. A later chapter in the book will tackle this topic.

As an organizational issue, employee supervision and evaluation has ascended in importance among criminal justice administrators. In fact, scholars have called into question the basic tenets of personnel supervision and evaluation that have dominated criminal justice organizations for many years (Goldstein, 1990). Most of these traditional efforts focused on "hard measures" of performance (e.g. arrests for police organizations) with very little concern over how these measures in any way related to larger organizational and societal objectives and goals (Bayley, 1991).

Current attempts at restructuring police organizations, court systems, and correctional organizations have centered on questions of how employees will be supervised and evaluated, as well as questions about the efficacy of newer methods to actually maintain control in these organizations (Skolnick and Bayley, 1986). Among criminal justice administrators, the question has become more direct and practical: How do I maintain control of employees such that their behaviors are consistent with organizational goals? A corollary question is what specific changes need to be implemented such that the supervision and evaluation of employees is more possible? Answers to these questions will be the focus of this chapter.

In addition, this chapter will examine contemporary methods and models of employee supervision and evaluation. The discussion presented will be guided by what goals and expectations we have for criminal justice organizations. Any examination of personnel supervision and evaluation must include an analysis of what goals we are seeking to achieve. As stated in chapter one, the goals of criminal justice are multiple, complex, and often times contradictory. As such, to talk about the supervision and evaluation of criminal justice employees we must include a specific set of goal contexts that focus our understanding. We will begin the discussion with the idea of multiple goals, goal consensus and criminal justice administration, move to an examination of structural aspects of criminal justice organizations, explore models of employee supervision and evaluation, and conclude with a commentary on the efficacy of these ideas as they relate to the administration and management of criminal justice organizations.

Learning Objectives
When finished studying this chapter the reader will be able to:

1. Define the major differences between the traditional model of employee supervision and the human service model of employee supervision.

2. Define centralization, formalization and complexity in relation to organizational structure and employee supervision.

3. Define the five major elements of the traditional model of employee supervision.

4. Identify three reasons to implement of the human service model of employee supervision.

5. Discuss why and why not the human service model of employee supervision could be implemented in criminal justice organizations.

Key Terms

Goal Consensus
Centralization
Complexity
Decentralization
Unity Of Command
Authority Rulification
Sharing of Power
Participative Management

Spatial Dispersion
Formalization
Differentiation
Span Of Control
Clear Delegation Of Specialization
Vertical Differentiation
Horizontal Differentiation

Chapter Outline

I. Criminal Justice Administration: The Search For Goal Consensus
    A. It is a common and widely held belief that criminal justice organizations are expected to provide multiple services to the community.
        1. All components of the criminal justice system have multiple goals and functions.
        2. These goals contradict one another and it is difficult to discern the primary direction of the organization.
        3. The police role is multidimensional and often times involves conflict as to the primacy of goals.
    B. For criminal justice administrators the central objective is to determine the goals of their communities and the most efficient ways to meet those goals.
        1. In communities where populations are diverse and large arriving at goal consensus on what the local system of criminal justice should be accomplishing is no small task.
        2. This is why the rank-and-file worker, whether it be a police officer on the beat or a correctional officer in a prison, is the most important part of the administration and management of criminal justice organizations.

II. Organizational Structure And Employee Supervision
    A. Organization structure is central to the understanding of employee.
        1. It is impossible to discuss the process issues of leadership, motivation, power, decision-making, supervision, and employee evaluation without first examining organizational structure.
    B. Richard Hall (1987) offers a model of understanding organizational structure by exploring the three fundamental dimensions: centralization, formalization, and complexity.
        1. Centralization refers to the degree to which power and authority are concentrated at the higher levels of the organization.
        2. Formalization is the extent to which the organization's structure and procedures are formally established through rules and regulations.
            a. Public organizations must develop policies and procedures that direct and guide their employees toward the accomplishment of public goals.
            b. Organizations of criminal justice are expected to be formalized due in large measure to the issue of public accountability.
            c. Formalization is often times expressed through the presence

of rule books and operating procedural manuals
- d. Litigation in recent years has forced criminal justice administrators to become more sensitive to the importance of rules and regulations in the supervision and direction provided employee.
3. Complexity is the number of subunits, levels, and specializations found in an organization.
   - a. Complexity is composed of three levels:
     (1) horizontal differentiation, the specialized division of labor across organizational unit
     (2) vertical differentiation, the number of positions located in the chain-of-command between the top officer and the rank-and-file employees
     (3) Spatial dispersion, the degree to which personnel are dispersed in space across both horizontal and vertical dimensions with the separation of power centers or tasks.
   - b. Differentiation, at both horizontal and vertical levels, makes it difficult for administrators and managers to supervise their employees employing old structures.
     (1) To provide greater supervision and control over personnel, differentiation is a likely outcome.

III. Centralization and Employee Supervision
   A. Decentralization within police organizations has meant allowing greater autonomy and authority over the decision-making among lower-level police employees, notably the police officer.
      1. Community-policing models stress the value of allowing individual police officers more autonomy to focus on unique problems they face in their communities.
      2. Traditional police hierarchy and bureaucracy is ineffective in addressing these community concerns according to critics.
      3. Decentralization requires greater autonomy for the police officer but also raises central questions about the relationship between officers and management.
         a. Mid-and upper-level managers will need to develop new methods of managing increased discretion.
         b. With this increased discretionary authority, police officers will require different models of supervision.
      4. Under the traditional method of managing jail inmates, officers were instructed to have minimal contact with prisoners. Direct supervision, by way of contrast, supports the idea that officers must be involved in the lives of the inmates.

           a. Officers are well trained and are situated within housing units with inmates, nothing separating them from the prisoners. They must rely on more complex intellectual skills such as reasoning and interpersonal communication to be effective in their jobs.
           b. Officers are given greater responsibilities for the planning, coordinating, and completion of tasks.
              (1) This is known as vertical loading (See chapter 5)
    5. Decentralization remains controversial for the criminal justice administrator. Since the primary rationale for bureaucratic approaches to criminal justice management has been greater.

IV. Formalization, or the degree to which the organization is controlled by written policies and procedures, is a constant for all criminal justice organizations.
    1. Clear examples are police departments and correctional organizations where policies and procedures serve as the basis upon which the organizations function.
    2. Out of concern for accountability, public organization routinely increase the degree to which they are formalized.

V. Complexity and Employee Supervision
    A. Centralization stresses the degree to which authority, specifically decisionmaking authority, is shared among employees, complexity refers to the "tallness" or "flatness" of an organization.
    B. Tall organizations, such as evidenced within many criminal justice agencies, make direct employee supervision a difficult task.
        1. It is very difficult for police supervisors to know exactly how, when, and where officers are performing their duties.
        2. The central problem of police supervision exists at the front-line level between sergeant and officer.
        3. The police sergeant is not able to visibly inspect and supervise his/her charges in a direct way.
        4. Instead, what is typically employed is a supervision style that relies heavily upon negotiation and compromise between officer and police supervisor.
    C. The complexity issue has surfaced in discussions how tall organizations are able to accomplish police objectives, while remaining sensitive to competing demands in the community.

VI. The Traditional Model of Employee Supervision
- A. The traditional model of employee supervision stresses centralized authority, clear-cut rules and regulations, well developed policies and procedures, and discernable lines of authority operationalized through a chain of command.
- B. The traditional model stresses high degrees of centralization, formalization, and complexity.
  1. Contemporary critics, however, question the effectiveness and appropriateness of this model to the changing societal expectations of the criminal justice system.
- C. The traditional model is made up of the following elements: a hierarchy that stresses an identifiable span of control, a precise unity of command, and a clear delegation of authority; rulification; and specialization of services and activities of employees (Gaines, Southerland, and Angell, 1991).
- D. Span of control refers to the appropriate number of employees that can be managed by any one supervisor.
  1. Span of control is a central question in the delivery of services to probationers and parolees (McShane and Krause, 1993).
  2. For police departments, span of control refers to the number of officers than can be reasonably monitored by a supervisor.
- E. Unity of command refers to the placement of one person in charge of a situation and an employee.
  1. For control and supervision to be maximized, there has to be one supervisor, known by every employee.
- F. Delegation of authority maintains the integrity of the organization by clearly defining tasks and responsibilities of employees, as well as delegating power and authority to complete tasks.
  1. Each employee understands his/her role in the accomplishment of tasks and where they fit into the goals of the organization.
- G. Rulification emphasizes the importance of rules and regulations to the organization.
  1. Every policy, procedure, and directive must have some specific written referent.
  2. As a control mechanism, rules, policies, and procedures are the essential components of the organization.
- H. Specialization involves the division of labor in the organization.
  1. Each employee knows his/her tasks and is held accountable to those tasks.
  2. Through specialization, employee supervision is enhanced, since it is through exact job definition that employees can be evaluated, disciplined, promoted, and dismissed

VII. Human Service Model of Employee Supervision
  A. The human service model views the supervision process within the context of both individual employee goals, as well as larger organizational goals.
    1. The human service model attempts to integrate employee goals into organizational goals.
  B. Toch (1978) states: less bureaucracy is a central tenet of the human - service model of employee supervision.
    1. The human - service model approach stresses the importance of decentralization of authority for greater decision-making capabilities among lower level members, fewer rules to encumber the enlarged activities of employees, and breaking down of the traditional hierarchy found in most police and correctional organizations.
  C. Peters and Waterman (1982) stress autonomy and entrepreneurship (less centralization), simultaneous loose-tight properties (less formalization), and simple form, lean staff (less complexity).
  D. Goldstein (1990) reports a new supervision model in police organizations requires a decentralization of authority supports a model that is able to integrate the knowledge and concerns of officers into a coherent and strategic plan to deal with community problems, such as crime.
  E. Wright (1995) offers identical prescriptions for correctional administrators and managers. He suggests that correctional institutions can be made more cohesive and work toward both organizational goals as well as developing people in the organization.
    1. His ideas center around three fundamental concepts: employee ownership, delegation, and the sharing of power.
    2. Employee ownership refers to the ability to have a greater voice in the creation of institutional policy, "People who 'own' their job and 'own' their organization feel strong, capable, and committed."
    3. Delegation allows employees the opportunities to make decisions that affect their ability to perform tasks.
    4. Sharing of power is given to employees to enhance their performance levels and adjust to contingencies of the institutional environment.
  F. The fundamental difference between the traditional model and the human service model is the control of the employee versus a primary emphasis is on the completion of organizational tasks.

Exercise

This questionnaire was developed by criminal justice practitioners during training sessions at the National Academy of Corrections and it has been tested for its validity. The situations, the scoring, and the theory have been patterned after Hersey and Blanchard's Situational Leadership. These authors based their efforts on the Contingency Management Theory which is described in Chapter 7.

- The situations and possible answers are designed so that there is a best answer for each situation, a second best answer, a poor answer, and a very poor answer.

- The situations are equally divided so that there are six best <u>Directive</u> answers, six best <u>Coaching</u> answers, six best <u>Supportive</u> answers, and six best <u>Delegating</u> answers. A page of the questionnaire instructions describes these leadership and decision making styles.

- The students should answer the situations individually and they should try to select the correct answer based on their knowledge now that they have completed the first two sections of the text.

- Scoring the questionnaire will reveal the students' tendency to prefer one style over another and which styles they do not prefer. The scoring should also show how accurate they were in selecting the best answers.

- Allow approximately 20-30 minutes for students to complete the instrument. The process of administering the instrument and the following discussion may consume two or more hours.

- When the scoring in completed, lead a discussion of the issues of employee supervision. The content of Chapters 7 and 8 is specifically related to the theory of situational leadership and the discussions should be lengthy and in depth. The instrument should serve as a capstone for the first two sections of the text.

The instrument is located in the appendices of this manual.

Part III   Group Behavior in Criminal Justice Organizations

Chapter 9
Occupational Socialization

Chapter Overview

An organization is more than a collection of individuals. Organizations influence the people within them in both formal and informal ways. The interactions of individuals of equal status within the organization, communication along, hierarchical lines, and contact between workers in criminal justice and offenders or the general public all contribute to the culture and ethos of criminal justice organizations. In this field, theory and research have looked beyond the individual to group influences to explain such problems as conflict, corruption, and the abuse of power. In Part Three we examine the role of the group within criminal justice organizations. We consider how groups shape what goes on and how managers can influence that process.

In this chapter we examine the process by which recruits in the occupations of criminal justice become seasoned. We examine the socialization influences on judges. parole officers, and other criminal justice professionals from both a theoretical and practical perspective. We also consider difficulties in the socialization process that may contribute to such problems as stress or misconduct. In particular, we review the research on the socialization of police and corrections officers. We focus on recruitment as well as formal and informal training practices. Finally, we consider the ways in which managers influence the process of socialization in criminal justice organizations.

Learning Objectives

When finished studying this chapter the reader will be able to:

1. Discuss the major influences of occupational socialization on the criminal justice system.
2. Describe organizational culture.
3. Define the socialization process.
4. Discuss the problems in the socialization process.
5. List and discuss strategies for socialization.

Key Terms

Occupational Socialization
Corruption
Organizational Culture
Values
Norms
Folkways
Mores

Social Or Informal Sanctions
Anticipatory Stage
"escalation episodes"
Role Conflict
Model Of Influences
Socialization Process
Codified Mores

Chapter Outline

I. Occupational socialization is the process by which a person acquires the values, attitudes, and behaviors of an ongoing occupational social system.
   A. It is a continuous process and includes both intentional influences, such as training, and unintentional influences, such as the locker-room or work-group culture.
   B. The attitudes, values, and behaviors acquired as a result of occupational socialization can include those regarded as appropriate and legitimate for the job as well as those that are illegitimate.
   C. Thus judges may learn appropriate sentence lengths for offender, but judges convicted in the 1986-1988 Greylord investigations in Chicago argued that they also learned to accept bribes because of the shared view that they were underpaid compared with their lawyer peers.
   D. Behaviors of individuals in organizations, for better or for worse, persists as long as the attitudes, beliefs, perceptions, habits, and expectations of organizational members remain constant.
      a. This consistency is particularly evident in criminal justice organizations.
      b. The practices of police officers and prison staff often seem unchanging and even resistant to change efforts.
      c. One common assessment of legal efforts to change criminal justice organizations is that the courts seem more efficient at bringing about procedural than substantive change.
      d. Katz and Kahn (1978) give the social-psychological concept of role a central place in their theory of organizations.
      e. Organizations are best understood as systems of roles. These roles link the individual to the organization and assure its continuity.

II. Organizational Culture
- A. Culture can be briefly described as a set of assumptions, values and beliefs shared by members of an organization.
    1. The assumptions, values and beliefs create language, symbols and folklore and ultimately serve to direct the behaviors of the organizational members, especially in response to work related problems.
    2. Edgar Schein (1985) summarizes common meanings of organizational culture. Common meanings include observed behavioral regularities, such as language, patterns of interactions, rituals, norms that evolve in working groups.
    3. Dominant values espoused by an organization such as rehabilitation, crime prevention, the philosophy of the organization toward employees or clients, rules of the game for getting along in the organization's social system and the feeling or climate created in an organization be the way employees are managed or interact.
    4. A pattern of basic assumptions -invented, discovered, or developed by a group as it reams to cope with its problems of external adaptation and internal integration -- that has worked well enough to be considered valid to be taught to new members as the correct way to perceive, think, and feel in relation to those problems" (Schein, 1985).
    5. The process of socialization in an organization serves to impose the organization's patterns of basic assumptions upon its new members.
- B. Culture is often defined as the complex whole of a society and includes knowledge, belief, art, laws, morals, customs and other capabilities and routines acquired by the members (Tylor, 1958).
- C. Cultural patterns evolve to provide a ready made solution. This does not mean that it is the best or only solution, but that the culture develops a set of standard patterns for dealing with common problems
    1. The more a society relies upon its ready made solutions, the more deeply entrenched the culture.
- D. Societies develop language to solve the problem of communicating and it becomes the frame work for its culture.
    1. Groups also have desirable goals which are expressed as values.
    2. Norms evolve that specify what people should or shouldn't do
    3. Folkways, standard ways of doing things, mores, strong views of right and wrong and laws, codified mores enforced by the group, evolve.
    4. Once a society or group has developed its culture it attempts to perpetuate the culture.

III. The Socialization Process
- A. Stages of Socialization
    1. The socialization literature generally divides the process of change into three distinct stages: anticipatory, formal, and informal.
    2. The socialization process begins prior to the entry of an individual into an occupation. In this anticipatory stage, those considering a particular field begin to anticipate the demands and expectations of their future job.
        a. They begin to adopt attitudes and values they believe are consistent with the occupation, and they come to view themselves as members of a group.
        b. During this stage, individuals are influenced by two main reference groups. First, those tangential to the occupation, may transmit their views of the job. Second, members of the occupation may directly transmit information about the job.
    3. When a person joins a particular occupation, the second, or formal, stage in socialization usually occurs. This is generally a period of formalized training.
    4. The third and ongoing phase of socialization is the informal stage.
        a. In this stage the relevant reference group is peers, managers, and even clients to whom a worker is exposed on a daily basis. Here the routine of the job shapes the role of the criminal justice worker.
- B. A Model of Influences
    1. A theoretical model of the process of taking organizational roles has been detailed by Katz and Kahn (1978). Their social-psychological model relies on four key concepts.
        a. <u>Role expectations</u> are the standards by which the behavior of an organizational member is judged. Different and even conflicting expectations may be held by supervisors, peers, clients, and even the general public.
        b. The <u>sent role</u> refers to the communication of those expectations to the member.
        c. The <u>received role</u> is the person's perception and understanding of the sent role.
        d. <u>Role behavior</u> is the person's response to the complex information received.
        e. According to this model, then, the behavior of an organizational member is the result of expectations communicated by significant others and filtered through his or her own psychological processes.

IV. Problems in the Socialization Process
   A. In criminal justice the most often discussed problem is that of role conflict.
      1. Role conflict is the occurrence of two or more role expectations such that compliance with one makes compliance with another difficult or impossible.
      2. Conflicting expectations may come from two or more role senders or may emanate from a single role sender.
      3. Lipsky (1980) argues that one of the defining characteristics of all street-level bureaucracies is competing goals.
         a. This competition is expressed in the conflicting expectations of front-line workers
         b. Police officers are charged with controlling crime as well as meeting due process constraints.
         c. Probation and parole officers must provide surveillance of their caseload to prevent crimes and assure compliance with rules, but they must also provide a supportive atmosphere and services to assist in adjustment to the community.
         d. All human service workers are sent conflicting messages about the process of their work. Although the importance of providing custodial or helping services is stressed, these services are to be provided to large caseloads of clients.
   B. Poole and Regoli (1980) concluded that role stress, defined as perceived uncertainty about job expectations, was positively associated with custodial orientation -- that is, those officers experiencing role ambiguity were likely to define their job in narrow custodial terms.
   C. Lee and Visano (1981) discuss a special case of role-related problems in criminal justice. These authors focus on the concept official deviance, which they define as "actions taken by officials which violate the law and/or the formal rules of the organization but which are clearly oriented toward the needs and goals of the organization, as perceived by the official, and thus fulfill certain informal rules of the organization" (1981).
      1. official deviance does not benefit the individual as corruption may but is aimed at furthering the perceived goals of the
   D. No aspect of criminal justice is immune to corruption.
      1. Investigations into corruption in the Cook County (Illinois) courts between 1986-1988 resulted in nearly sixty federal indictments for case fixing and payoffs.
      2. Probation officers have been known to exact sexual favors from clients who sought to avoid revocation.
      3. Corrections officers have been prosecuted for smuggling drugs into

prisons and even for aiding in prison escapes.
   4. Studies of police corruption have investigated behavior ranging from accepting an occasional free meal to participating in burglary rings.
  E. Sherman (1974) states that a rookie police officer's work group exercises considerable influence. The likelihood of new officers' accepting bribes is related to the extent lo which such practices already occur in the work group.
   1. There may also be supervisory support for corrupt practices.
   2. Corrupt police officers, however, do not view themselves as corrupt, and the sent role is viewed as one of non-deviance.
   3. Wilson (1968) points out that police justify some types of corruption by pointing to declining moral standards in the general community.
   4. Skolnick (1966) also explains that police officers legitimize some corrupt practices by distinguishing between practices that will or will not harm the public.
   5. Thus officers may differentiate between clean graft (acceptable) and dirty graft (unacceptable).

V. Strategies for Socialization
  A. Examination of the ways in which managers affect the process of socialization in criminal justice.
  B. A manager's impact at anticipatory state is generally limited and indirect.
   1. Managers can support what they regard as desirable images of the occupation.
  C. A direct influence on socialization occurs during recruitment and selection.
   1. The determination of job titles and qualifications is the first step in this process.
   2. Some communities, for example, use the title of police agent rather than police officer to convey a sense of professionalism.
   3. The change in title from prison guard to corrections officer was also meant to connote a different role for front-line prison staff.
   4. Campus security carries a different set of expectations than campus police, and state trooper conveys its own images.
  D Job qualifications also directly influence socialization.
   1. Experience, education, and even fitness requirements determine the paths candidates must take.
   2. In 1969 the Joint Commission on Correctional Manpower and Training noted that age requirements affected organizational roles by creating a generation gap between workers and clients in criminal justice.

3. A college education, now required for most social service positions, is regarded as beneficial for almost all entry-level positions in criminal justice (Waldron, 1984).
4. An obvious influence on organizational roles is exerted in the selection process itself. During this process a variety of criteria, often intuitive, sometimes systematic, is used to weed out candidates.
5. Efforts to introduce psychological assessments into the selection process are still more sophisticated but not necessarily more successful at discriminating good and bad employees.
6. A different approach is found in behavioral-skills assessments as a basis for selection.
   a. These assessments are based on job analyses and focus on the ability to perform specific tasks or tile potential to acquire necessary skills through training. Some criminal justice organizations are developing assessment centers that use simulations of on-the-job performance.

E. The formal stages of training provide significant opportunities to influence socialization.
   1. The process as well as the training content influence role taking.
   2. The degree of formalization is the extent to which training is segregated from the ongoing context of work.
   3. In criminal justice the police academy represents a highly formalized process, while most probation officers undergo a much less formalized process of onthejob training.

F. Formalization has several important consequences.
   1. The more formalized the more the training will stress adoption of appropriate attitudes and beliefs and the more new employees will be stigmatized in the organization, usually by segregating them in a rookie class.
   2. Collective socialization strategies involve the training of new members as a group.
   3. Individual strategies involve an apprenticeship approach to socialization.
   4. Collective strategies inevitably create feelings of comradeship and peer support as trainees experience being "in the same boat ."
   5. Individual strategies depend on the affective bonds between individuals and breed dependence on mentors or on established ways of doing things.

G. In sequential socialization a trainee passes through discrete stages on the way to becoming a fully accepted member of an organization.
   1. Police for example, go through a sequence of academy training, field training, and a probationary period, while corrections

officers frequently begin with onthejob training prior to entry into the academy.
   2. When training is divided into these relatively separate steps, coordination of those stages becomes important. Lack of coordination may mean that material is contradictory or that trainees can disregard material learned in one stage, as is often the case in the transition from training academy to onthejob training. This lack of continuity can lead to cynicism among the recruits.
H. Serial socialization relies on experienced veterans to groom newcomers in organizations. Criminal justice organizations frequently rely on serial practices.
   1. Experienced police officers, for example, often get academy instructor assignments and FTO jobs.
   2. Similarly, novice judges turn to experienced judges for advice.
   3. Such practices assure that organizations will change only slowly.
      a. Established attitudes and practices are passed on, and new ideas gain little support.
I. Investiture strategies make membership in organizations easy by accepting credentials as the major entrance requirements.
   1. Education and the practice of law will gain one entry to the judiciary and form the foundation for a professional identity. However, divestiture processes strip away certain characteristics before permitting entry.
J. Socialization is more prevalent during the early than the later stages of a career (Schein, 1971) and thus recruits are more susceptible than experienced workers.
   1. Personnel practices such as shift assignments or bidding procedures for job assignments may influence socialization.
   2. Klofas and Toch (1982) found that anti-inmate attitudes among young corrections officers received support when the rookies were clustered on the 3-to-11 shift. The officers lacked the seniority to bid on assignments that would have integrated them with their experienced peers on desirable shifts.
K. Technological changes may also influence socialization.
   1. Continued training may alter expectations or relationships between employees and clients.
   2. Although socialization influences may be most prominent at the beginning of careers in criminal justice those influences should not be neglected at any time.

Exercise

Students: In your small groups answer the issues concerning the case. Consider the chapter objectives, key words and the outline. The case is in the text in Chapter 9.

Case Study - Reflections on a Career

I struggled through all of the crap in law school to join the noblest of professions, I thought. I had a belief in the system of justice, that through the adversarial process, the truth would be discovered and justice would be served. I knew about plea bargaining, but I was totally naive about the legal system and how the "old boys" ran things. I passed the bar exam and joined a decent law firm. I was intent on being a defense attorney. The state had a skilled staff of prosecuting attorneys and had the power of skilled detectives to work with to get convictions. To have a balanced advisarial process, skilled and dedicated defense attorneys were important. Then, I got my first case.

The court appointed my firm to represent an individual who had earned a solid criminal record and was indigent. My boss was happy to assign the case to me to prime the pump as he put it. Negotiate the best plea you can for your client, was his advice. The defendant had served time and did not seem troubled by the possibility of returning to prison. However, he maintained his innocence and was apposed to accepting a plea. I discussed the case with the prosecutor assigned to it and asked to look over the file. I was treated well, but clearly as a beginner. As I perused the file, I noted and commented on several discrepancies in the case. The tone of our conversation changed and the prosecutor became somewhat miffed about my analysis. I patiently pressed my point of view. However, the chief prosecutor, who was in ear shot of our conversation intervened. She made it strikingly clear that this was a plea bargain case. She firmly explained that my client had committed a string of burglaries over the years, that this offense fit his pattern, that everyone knew it was his job and we didn't need to expend time and money agonizing over discrepancies in the case. She further explained the I was assigned the case as a personal favor to allow me to get some experience with the system and make a few easy bucks. By this time she was in my face lecturing me about waking up and forgetting all of the crap I had learned in high school civics or law school. This put me over the edge. I asked for my copy of the file and told her and her assistant that I would see them in court.

To make a long story short, I took the case to a jury trial and obtained a not guilty verdict. Along the way, I embarrassed the investigating detective who was not well prepared for the obvious plea bargain case, angered the judge who, as I later found out, thought my client was guilty as sin and completely alienated the chief prosecutor and her assistant who tried the case. My boss attempted mend the few fences I broke and asked me to apologize and be gracious with the people I had beat up in the process. I was stunned and outraged. The jury found my client not guilty, therefore, in my mind, that was the truth. The adversarial process should prevail over egos or convenience, I thought. I stood my idealistic ground and refused to apologize to anyone. A month after the acquittal, my client committed another burglary, was appointed another attorney although he requested I represent him, pleaded guilty to a lessor offense and was sentenced to prison. Two months latter, I was asked to resign from my law firm and advised to practice on my own.

Well, I still do criminal defense work and the thieves and convicts love me. But they usually can't pay their fees. I have to pay the rent and my bills, so I developed a pretty good divorce practice. But the real truth is that most of my domestic relations clients can't afford to go to court and have the other truth found through the adversarial process. So, we bargain and settle.

Case Study Questions:

1. Describe the occupational socialization process illuminated in the case study.

2. What major weaknesses appear to exist in the stages of socialization?

3. Identify the stages of socialization that occurred to the writer.

4. What are the major problems that are solved by the criminal legal system that create the rules of the game?

Chapter 10
Power and Political Behavior

Chapter Overview

The concept of power is expressed in different forms within the various components of the criminal justice system. Whether it be the sentencing judge, the police sergeant, a prisoner, or a correctional administrator, all rely on power to gain compliance from others and are affected by power relationships. A police supervisor may wish to exercise control over the beat cop, or a prisoner may desire to control another prisoner. Expressions of power are widespread in criminal justice organizations. In addition, who has power and how that power is acquired vary within the different components of criminal justice. Moreover, power and politics are inseparable in the criminal justice system. To the chagrin of some criminal justice employees. often times they feel that power is used inappropriately and to the detriment of their organization. This is when power is viewed as a political expression. The consequences of such perceptions can be injurious to the organization, something we will examine later in the chapter. Suffice it to say that expressions of power - and consequences of these expressions - are pervasive in criminal justice organizations.

Police organizations, for example, employ different types of power to gain compliance from officers. The types of power used depend on the tasks and functions of the particular unit. Supervisors in the vice unit do not use the same types of power as those in the detective unit because each unit has its own duties and responsibilities. In correctional systems, the types of power used by supervisory personnel are often constrained by a number of factors inherent in the prison structure. As an example, we know that pure coercive power rarely works in prison. in part, because inmates significantly outnumber staff. As a result, we see others types of power used by corrections administrators and officers to gain compliance from prisoners.

Our purpose in this chapter is to review the literature on the concept of power and apply this material to criminal justice organizations. A major goal of this chapter is to ascertain the types of power and authority employed in criminal justice bureaucracies by examining the major research that has been done in the criminal justice area. In addition, this chapter discusses the consequences of power relations in organizations and emphasizes the political nature of power in organizations and the strategies criminal justice officials can employ to maintain their power positions.

Learning Objectives

When finished studying this chapter the reader will be able to:

1. Define power in organizations from three perspectives.
2. List and describe three types of authority.
3. List and describe the five bases of power according to French and Raven.
4. Discuss the most significant types of positive power in criminal justice organizations.
5. List and describe four personality traits affecting an administrator's approach to organizational political behavior.

Key Terms

Traditional Authority
Charismatic Authority
Legal Authority
Reward Power
Coercive Power
Legitimate Power
Referent Power
Expert Power

The need for power
Machiavellianism
Locus of control
Risk-seeking propensity
Political behavior
Power recipient
Power holder
Cognitive structure

Chapter Outline

I. Power Defined
   A. Power is one of the most difficult concepts to define, and, as a result, the organizational literature contains multiple definitions of it.
   B. If we view organizational power as l a product of exchange relationships in organizations, we can see how the interdependent nature of organizational tasks creates power for some people.
   C. Specific units within an organization are able to exhibit what is known as "interdepartmental power".
   D. Criminal justice organizations generally operate in consistent and predictable ways.
      1. What is important to criminal justice organizations is that they accomplish their tasks in an efficient manner while simultaneously meeting the demands of the public.
   E. Summary of the key aspects of power in organizations is as follows:

1. First, power: denotes that "a person or group of persons or organization of persons determines or affects, what another person or group or organization will do" (Tannenbaum, 1962).
2. Second, power exists among the units of an organization as well as at the interpersonal level.
3. Third, power in an organization depends on how subunits deal with uncertainty and on whether they meet the criteria of substitutability and centrality.
4. Finally, we differentiate between power and authority. Many have considered these terms interchangeable, but doing so is not helpful to an understanding of the process of power acquisition in organizations.

II. Types of Power and Authority
   A. Weber delineated three types of authority:
      1. Traditional, Charismatic, and Legal.
      2. <u>Traditional authority</u> is authority that is vested in the position a person holds and that has a long tradition in a culture or organization.
      3. The second type of authority is <u>charismatic authority</u>. This type is founded in the personable attributes or actions (or both) of a particular individual in an organization.
      4. Finally, there is <u>legal authority</u>. This type of authority is based on an appeal to the formal rules and regulations of an organization. In addition, this type of authority is rooted in the hierarchy. It is predicated on the belief that subordinates are expected to follow the orders and commands of those above them in the formal chain of command.
   B. French and Raven (1968) theorize that there are five bases of power in organizations. The five types of power are reward, coercive, legitimate, referent, and expert. The person who expresses the power is referred to as a power holder, while the receiver of the power is referred to as a power recipient
      1. <u>Reward power</u> is based on the perception of the power recipient that the power holder can grant some type of reward or remuneration for compliance to orders or commands.
      2. <u>Coercive power</u> is based on the belief of subordinates that if they do not do as they are told they will be either threatened with punishment or punished directly.
      3. <u>Legitimate power</u> is exercised when a power holder is able to influence a power recipient to do something based on some internalized belief of the power recipient. This type of power is

most closely aligned to Weber's concept of authority.
   4. <u>Referent power</u> is based on the identification of the power holder with the power recipient. This power is predicated on the attractiveness of the power recipient to the power holder.
   5. <u>Expert power</u> is based on the power recipient's belief that the power holder has a high level of expertise in a given area. This type of power is based on the "cognitive structure" of the power recipient and fosters the dependence of the power recipient on the power holder.
C. Bacharach and Lawler (1980) suggest information as another source of power in organizations. Individuals or groups may have power because of their ability to control the information flow in the organization.
   1. This power can be distinguished from expert power because it is derived from one's position and not from one's knowledge.
D. Salancik and Pfeffer (1974) have shown how certain subunits in organizations become powerful because of their ability to acquire critical resources. They suggested that subunit power is contingent largely on the ability of the subunit or department to gain outside grant and contract funds.

III. Consequences of Power Relations
   A. Lord (1977 analyzed the relationship between types of social power and leadership functions. Lord concludes that legitimate power is highly related to the leadership functions of developing orientation (providing direction to employees), communicating, and coordinating, whereas coercive power is most highly related to facilitating evaluations, proposing solutions, and total functional behavior.
   B. Julian (1966) concludes that different types of power are utilized.. An implication from this research is that differing organizations use diverse types of power to accomplish their organizational goals.

IV. The Legitimacy of Power and Political Behavior
   A. According to Tosi, Rizzo, and Carroll (1986:527), "when legitimate authority fails, political behavior arises."
      1. Political behavior is any action of the criminal justice worker that promotes individual goals over organizational goals. In their opinion, political behavior exists in when there is:
         a. a lack of consensus among members about goals,
         b. disagreement over the means to achieve goals, or
         c. anxiety about resource allocation.
   B. Dalton (1959) suggests that with the diffusion of types of power in organizations there is a concomitant rise of powerful cliques or

coalitions. These cliques defend their members in response to various threats to organizational autonomy.
   1. Pfeffer (1981) points out that such cliques and coalitions are highly political, relying on various strategies to advance their own purposes and causes over those of other coalitions in the organization.
C. Hellriegel, Slocum, and Woodman (1995) suggest that there are personality traits among certain people that make them more prone to exercising political behaviors in organizations. These four personality traits are: the need for power, Machiavellianism, locus of control, and risk-seeking propensity.
   1. The need for power is a common trait among both effective and non-effective leaders. Leaders who seek to simply dominate others through expressions of power will create climates where political behavior is more likely than those leaders who seek power to move employees toward some identifiable and acceptable levels of performance.
   2. Machiavellianism is predicated on the ideas of manipulation and deceit. Administrators who exhibit this trait view political behavior as a prerequisite to effective leadership. Such a trait accentuates manipulation of employees for specific ends. Such a trait, in the long run, perpetuates greater division among employees and between employees and administrators.
   3. Locus of control refers to individuals who have a high internal locus rather than external locus concerning their ability to control their fates within organizations. A high internal locus within persons means that they believe they are able to control and influence people and their surroundings.
   4. Individuals with a high propensity for risk-taking are much more likely to engage in political behavior than those individuals with a low risk-taking personality. These persons view risk-taking as a necessity within a politically charged organization. They enjoy taking the risks and the political behavior that is a necessary element of taking risks.

V. Effective Types of Power
   A. The exercise of legitimate, charismatic, and expert power leads to acceptance on the part of the employee; reward and coercive power may lead to acceptance if the power is used for some legitimate purpose.
   B. Legitimate, charismatic, and expert bases of power lead to acceptance on the part of employees, acceptance leads to the rationalization and justification of the behavior.

Exercise

Students: In your small groups answer the issues concerning the case. Consider the chapter objectives, key words and the outline. The case is in Chapter 10 in the text.

Case Study
The Corrections Officer's Dilemma:
Who Has the Power in the Joint?

Nantucket Prison was built well before the beginning of the nineteenth century. It was the end-of-the-line prison in a state correctional system that was overcrowded and under funded. Besides housing some 200 inmates above its rated capacity, the prison was run by gangs with such authority that corrections officers often feared for their lives and did not have any ideas on how to interact with them effectively. This situation changed when veteran Robert Stones was transferred from the state's small camp system to the prison. Stones had been in corrections for almost twenty years and understood how to deal with inmates or, in his words, 'deal with the inmate mentality.' He was viewed by Warden Johnson as someone who could train the corrections officers how to deal effectively with inmates.

The corrections officers were hesitant and somewhat uncertain about what Stones could teach them that they did not already know. Stones agreed that his real value to the institution would be training the new officers. Warden Johnson agreed that Stones should work with the young corps of officers who were receptive to his ideas of dealing with inmates. The first corrections officer assigned to work with Stones was a new recruit named James Bowers. Bowers had a background in community based corrections and knew about how former inmates, those on parole, reacted to authority. Because much of what he knew was community oriented, Stones wondered whether Bowers understood what prison life was about, even though he had been to prison transporting parolees who had their paroles revoked. Knowing that what Bowers learned he would tell the other officers, Stones was methodical in his training.

'The first thing you have to remember, Bowers, is that prisoners run the joint,' said Stones. 'Even more important is the fact that inmates could take over a prison any time they wanted, and that is why you have to understand where the powerful inmates are coming from.' Bowers was somewhat bewildered by Stones's statement. He asked, 'If inmates run the prison, what the hell kind of role do corrections officers have in this process? What are we just baby sitters for these guys?' with a smile on his face, Stones responded, 'Well, to a degree, and with some inmates we are nothing but baby sitters. But the important point is that you have to recognize that inmates do have a say about their incarceration. Forget the idea that we have total power here. Most of what we do is compromising. You got to compromise.' Bowers did not know how to respond, but he remembered Stones's suggestions and thought them over.

Three months later he had his first chance to use them. It was an ordinary day in cellblock C when Officer Bowers noticed three inmates cornered in the maintenance room. His initial response was to go over and break up the inmates, Seeing what Bowers was going to do, Stones stopped him and suggested that he make sure other inmates in the cellblock were ready for lunch. Later in the day Bowers asked Stones why he prevented him from breaking up the inmates. Stones responded, 'Those three inmates were making a deal for some marijuana, and the white guy was the dealer. He has a lot of power in here, and I respect him and his position.' He added, 'He distributes the dope, and I let him, while at the some time he controls the disruptive inmates in the block. We have our little deals that keep this place running. Now I want you to know that it's not a lot of dope, just enough to keep the prisoners happy.' Bowers could not believe what he had heard. He angrily responded, 'How can you let such things go on in the prison? We have to have greater control.' With a grin on his face, Stones replied, 'We have control because of what I do. It gets back to what I said earlier, that you have to respect the fact that some inmates have power in this prison and that pushing dope is one type of activity that gives them power.' Bowers responded that he thought this type of dealing with inmates was in the long run dangerous because it caused fights and violence among prisoners. But Stones reaffirmed that his dealing with powerful inmates who distributed marijuana was essential to the stability of the prison. He added that control problems with inmates in the past were related to the inability of officers to recognize the power that prisoners have in the prison and that power can be expressed in a number of ways, including the selling of dope.

'Now I don't want you to get the wrong idea,' said Stones. 'I don't think that we should let these guys do whatever they want in here, but there has to be a recognition by the officers that dope peddling gives some guys a lot of power and that it has been in prison for a long time and will continue to be around. The fact is that we can't get rid of all of it; we can only hope to control it. The same is true of those religious leaders in here. Do you think those Muslim leaders get what they want from these other inmates and officers? You bet they do, and it's all because they are respected by a lot of the inmates. To do our jobs, we have to deal with the realities of the prison.' Officer Bowers responded, 'Is it the same way with the gang leaders in here?' 'Now you are catching on kid. It's like the inmates say, you have to give a man respect if you want respect from him,' answered Stones.

Officer Bowers went home that night and thought through what Officer Stones had said to him. He concluded that prison stability may depend not only on the power of inmates but also on how officers use their own power among inmates. Later that night a statement Stones had made to him three months earlier rang through his head: 'Remember, Bowers, inmates run the joint.'

Case Study Questions

1. What types of power do you believe would be the most effective in gaining control of Nantucket Prison?

2. Do you think Stones is effective as a corrections officer in his interaction with prisoners? If so, why? If not, why not?

3. What are some problems with negotiating with prisoners to maintain control of a prison? Will negotiating give corrections officers increased legitimacy among prisoners? Is that good or bad for the prison? Why or why not?

Chapter 11
Organizational Conflict

Chapter Overview

This chapter addresses a subject that many academics, practitioners, and policymakers interested in criminal justice find perplexing - the process of conflict in criminal justice organizations. We have all worked in organizations and have experienced conflict, whether it be disagreement with the boss about our work assignment or about the overall direction of the organization. Conflict is endemic to all organizations, including the organizations of criminal justice. This chapter examines conflict in criminal justice organizations by exploring several topics.

First, we provide a definition of conflict in organizations, along with an examination of the stages of a conflict episode. We describe what conflict in criminal justice organizations means and, more importantly, the process of conflict. We should then be able to understand why conflict exists in the organizations of criminal justice and the many dynamics associated with the conflict process. Second, we explore the types of conflict behaviors exhibited by people in organizations. In this section of the chapter, our discussion focuses on existing knowledge from organizational - behavior literature about the process of conflict in organizations and applies these ideas to the operations of criminal justice organizations. Third, we examine the topic of conflict management. Various interventions are suggested, and various dimensions of the outcome of a conflict are explored. We suggest also that a proper analysis of conflict and its resolution must consider how conflict reaches well beyond the borders of the individual organizations of criminal justice. Finally, the chapter concludes with a discussion of the role of conflict in criminal justice organizations and how conflict management can enhance the effectiveness of these organizations.

The conditions of conflict can include, first, resource scarcity and policy differences. Second, conflict can be understood as producing affective states within individuals. Third, conflict can be viewed from the cognitive states of the individual employee. Fourth, conflict in organizations has been examined by exploring the actual conflict behavior, whether it is passive resistance or outright confrontational or aggressive behavior.

Learning Objectives

When finished studying this chapter the reader will be able to:

1. List and briefly discuss the four types of conflict in organizations.

2. List and briefly discuss the five stages of a conflict episode.

3. List and briefly discuss the five types of conflict behavior.

4. List and briefly discuss the two types of Conflict Management.

Key Terms

Personal Conflict	Cooperativeness
Group Conflict	Assertiveness
Intra-organizational Conflict	Competing Behavior
Vertical Conflict	Accommodating Behavior
Horizontal Conflict	Avoiding Behavior
Line staff Conflict	Collaborating Behavior
Role Conflict	Compromising Behavior
Inter-organizational Conflict	Process Interventions
Latent Conflict	Contextual-Modification
Perceived Conflict	Structural Interventions
Felt Conflict	Constituent Pressure
Manifest Conflict	Selection and Training Interventions
Conflict Aftermath	Personal Characteristics

Chapter Outline

I. Types of Conflict
    A. We can identify four types of conflict in organizations, each of which requires a different adjustment mechanism. The four types of conflict are personal conflict, group conflict, intra-organizational conflict, and inter-organizational conflict.
        1. Personal Conflict - This type of conflict exists within the individual and usually is some form of goal conflict or cognitive conflict. Typically, this form of conflict is a result of not meeting one's expectations.
        2. Group Conflict - Group conflict occurs in organizations when individual members disagree on some point of interest.
        3. Intra-organizational Conflict - intra-organizational conflict is generated by the structural makeup of an organization-that is, by formal authority in the organization and how it is delegated. There are four major types of intra-organizational conflict:
        a. vertical conflict

        b. horizontal conflict
        c. line staff conflict
        d. role conflict
  B. Inter-organizational Conflict - Inter-organizational conflict occurs when there is a common purpose among different organizational units but disagreement as how that purpose will be achieved. This type of conflict arises when a separate organizational unit (such as one component of the criminal justice system) perceives its goals and obJectives to be in conflict with those of other units.

II. Stages of a Conflict Episode
  A. The five stages of a conflict episode are: latent conflict, perceived conflict, felt conflict, manifest conflict, and conflict aftermath.
    1. Latent Conflict - This stage of the conflict occurs when the conditions that are the underlying sources of the conflict are present. According to Pondy (1985), latent conflict is typically rooted in competition for scarce resources, drives for autonomy, or divergence of subunit goals.
    2. Perceived Conflict - This stage of the conflict episode occurs when at least one of the two parties recognize that a conflict situation exists. When they do, they may seek to escalate the conflict episode or choose to deflect it.
    3. Felt Conflict - Felt conflict occurs when a party personalizes the conflict situation.
    4. Manifest Conflict - This stage of the conflict episode is characterized by overt or covert behavior to bring out the conflict. In prisons, for example, manifest conflict may be expressed in riots or disturbances.
    5. Conflict Aftermath - At this point in the conflict episode, if the antecedent conditions (competition for scarce resources, drives for autonomy, and divergent subunit goals) are dealt with in a satisfactory manner, the conflict will dissolve.

III. Conflict Behaviors
  A. Awareness of conflict behaviors is important to our understanding of the role conflict plays in criminal justice organizations and it enables managers to implement effective conflict-management programs.
  B. Thomas (1985) reports conflict has two dimensions, each representing an individual's intention with respect to a conflict situation. The two dimensions are cooperativeness, attempting to satisfy the other party's concerns, and assertiveness, attempting to satisfy one's own concerns. Different combinations of these two dimensions can create

conflict behaviors.
1. Competing behavior (assertive, uncooperative) occurs when one is willing to place one's own concerns above the concerns of the other individual. Typically, force and even violence occur in this conflict situation. In addition, the competing type of conflict behavior seeks the resolution of the conflict in a fashion that maximizes one's own interests.
2. Accommodating behavior (unassertive, cooperative) satisfies the concerns of the other individual rather than one's own concerns in a conflict situation. This behavior may be quite rare in organizations because it is difficult to understand why one would neglect one's own interests and maximize another's, yet we all know this does happen in everyday life.
3. Avoiding behavior (unassertive, uncooperative) neglects both one's own concerns and the concerns of the other individual. People who exhibit avoiding behavior want a minimal amount of friction in their interactions and do everything in their power to make sure no problems occur between themselves and others.
4. Collaborating behavior (assertive, cooperative) attempts to satisfy the demands and concerns of both parties in a conflict situation; it is a type of conflict behavior that few possess yet many desire.
5. Compromising behavior (intermediate in both assertiveness and cooperativeness) seeks the middle ground. People who exhibit this type of conflict behavior realize that you cannot always get what you want and recognize that for the conflict to be resolved there must be some give and take by both sides.

IV. Conflict Management
   A. Process Interventions - These types of interventions fall into two categories.
      1. First, consciousness-raising interventions attempt to change the "internal experiences of the parties" that shape their behaviors.
      2. Second, interaction management occurs when a supervisor intervenes directly in the conflict situation between two subordinates, suggesting how the two parties can change their behaviors to resolve this conflict and avoid future conflicts.
   B. Personal characteristics - Our personalities affect how we deal with conflict.
   C. Informal rules - All organizations have written and unwritten rules about

how people are to behave. These rules are critical to the operation of the organization.
- D. Constituent pressure - In all organizations there is often pressure and competition among groups. This competition typically forces cohesiveness among the groups.
- E. Conflict of interest. According to Thomas (1985), this precursor exists in organizations when the concerns of two parties in an organization are incompatible. Such conflict is escalated when both parties are competing for limited resources.
- F. Power and status - Power and status play an important part in the conflicts that occur in organizations and their level of intensity.
- G. Organizational policy - An organizational policy is often created to minimize a conflict. However, if rules are nothing but the result of "political struggles" (Thomas, 1985), then one would expect that rules and organizational policies are only a short-term response.
- H. Structural Interventions - While process interventions are concerned with conflict episodes, structural interventions are designed to reduce conflict by examining and altering the conditions of the organization that promote conflict.
- I. Selection and training interventions - Selection interventions use screening procedures to choose the people who would be best for the organization and the job.
- J. Contextual-modification interventions - These types of interventions attempt to change the context within which parties interact. Such changes typically require forceful management and leadership in the policy-development process.

V. Limits to Conflict Management
- A. Although conflicts requiring contextual modification may be resolved, other conflicts are more intractable because managers have even less control over their resolution.
- B. Administrators have to accept that sometimes they will not be able to handle a conflict situation. Sometimes we fail in our attempts to deal with conflicts both internal and external to the organization. This failure, however, does not relegate us to doing nothing. The reasonable position is to learn from our mistakes and to go forward and resolve similar conflicts in the future with the knowledge gained from our past experiences.

VI. Is Conflict Management Possible in Criminal Justice Administration?
- A. According to Thomas (1985), successful conflict management deals with all the dimensions of conflict outcomes. There are three such dimensions:

1. First, is goal attainment by conflicting parties. In the conflict between treatment staff and custodial personnel, there has to be some type of goal attainment by either one group or the other or both.
2. Second, it would seem imperative that administrators in the criminal justice system be aware of the consequences of a conflict episode for the people involved. If, for example, treatment staff feel that they have been treated unfairly by the administration of the institution in resolving a conflict, this perception may adversely affect their productivity and outlook toward the job.
3. Third, conflict management in the criminal justice system must be economical of time and effort. An administrator of a state corrections system once said privately that his job entailed keeping the conflicts down in the department and keeping his name out of the newspapers. This example indicates the tremendous amount of effort put into dealing with conflicts both within the organizations of criminal justice and outside their boundaries.

VII. The Role of Conflict in Organizations
   A. Conflict in criminal justice organizations can be both beneficial and harmful. Much of the conflict that occurs in the components of the criminal justice system is good in the sense that it promotes change in those organizations. Conflict makes the system responsive to the demands of a changing environment.
   B. Conflict in criminal justice organizations seems inevitable given the fact of frequently incompatible goals. It is quite apparent that managers have to learn how to live with, adapt to, and cope with such conflict.

Exercise

Students: In your small groups answer the issues concerning the case. Consider the chapter objectives, key words and the outline. Apply the conflict resolution strategies to the Dogpatch County case from Chapter 7 and report on what Sheriff Dick Clark might do to resolve the issues. Identify a strategy that depicts:
   a Competing Behavior,
   an Accommodating Behavior,
   an Avoiding Behavior,
   a Collaborating Behavior,
   and a Compromising Behavior.

Part IV Processes in Criminal Justice Organizations

Chapter 12
Decision Making

Chapter Overview

Organizations pursue goals and accomplish tasks. These are complicated issues, but they are the issues that set organizations apart from individuals and groups. Managers must be concerned with how their organizations carry out those tasks and how well they perform. These are important concerns in criminal justice, where goals are often unclear and conflicting and where few unambiguous measures of accomplishment exist.

In Part IV the focus extends beyond the individual and group to the ways that organizations pursue their goals and accomplish their tasks. We first consider decision making within organizations, then the difficult process of determining the effectiveness of organizations. The final two chapters examine the process of change in criminal justice organizations and the role of research in these organizations.

Decision making is one of the most important concerns for managers in all organizations. Not only do they engage in this act directly, they also oversee the decisions of their subordinates. We see examples of good and bad decision making all the time. Part of the continued success of Johnson & Johnson has been attributed to the decision to keep Tylenol on the market under its original name despite the publicity about deaths from product tampering with cyanide in the early 1980s. However, the decision to change the formula for Coca-Cola in 1985 met with such resistance that the company had to bring "Classic Coke" back on the market. The space shuttle disaster in 1985 resulted in the death of seven astronauts and set back military and civilian space programs in the United States by three years. In criminal justice, decision making is no less important. Severe prison and jail overcrowding has been blamed on tensions that were based on faulty population projections. In 1984, the police decision to drop an incendiary bomb on the roof of a house to evict a cult in Philadelphia ultimately resulted in the burning of some sixty homes and creates a costly political firestorm.

Decision making in criminal justice extends well beyond the policy formulation process with its parallels in the business world. In criminal justice, countless decisions are made about the clients of the system. In the chapter, we examine the process of decision making In criminal justice.
We examine issues of theory and the growing recognition of the limits of rationality.

Next, the focus is on two issues in criminal justice decision making that appear to represent extremes in our assumptions about rationality. First, we investigate discretion in decision making, a topic often criticized by those seeking rational processes. Second, we study prediction, a topic often assumed to be linked to high degrees of rationality. These two issues have engendered more discussion in criminal justice than any other decision making topics. Finally, we consider the ways in which managers can influence the decision making process in criminal justice in an effort to increase rationality.

Learning Objectives

When finished studying this chapter the reader will be able to:

1. Define a decision and list important criminal justice factors relating to the definition.
2. List and briefly discuss the three significant kinds of information in the decision making process.
3. Define the "garbage can" theory of decision making.
4. List and briefly discuss the four types of criminal justice decision makers.
5. List and briefly discuss the five themes to improving criminal justice decisions.

Key Terms

"garbage can" theory
Consequences of Alternative
Cybernetic Decision Model
Satisfycing
Bounded Rationality
External Politics
Internal Politics
Sequentialists
Ah Yes! Decision Maker
The Simplifier

Numerical Weights
Decision Rules
Consistency in Theory
Performance Programs
Organizational Culture
Discretion
Prediction
Probability Estimates
Minimax Criteria
Ratifiers

Chapter Outline

I. Definition of a Decision
    A. A theory or broad framework guides most decisions.
        1. Complex decisions involve sophisticated theories.
    B. Goals in the decision making process are specific to each decision.
    C. Decision making involves three kinds of information.
        1. Alternatives need to be known.
        2. The consequences of Alternatives need to be known.
        3. Some information in needed about the subject of the decision to guide the selection of the alternatives.
    D. In criminal justice, many decisions rely on clinical decision rules, which are based on education, training, and experience.
    E. At the other extreme are decision rules involving the assignment of numerical weights to pieces of information. Those weights are added to produce a sum, which dictates the decision. Scales based on these principles have been developed for use in prosecution, bail, sentencing, and parole decisions.
    F. The processing of information according to decision rules produces outcomes.
    G. In a cybernetic, or self correcting, decision model the outcome of prior decisions provides feedback to influence future decisions.
        1. Cybernetic decision processes are based on mechanical models similar to the thermostat in a house.
        2. Feedback may affect future decisions through its influence on theory, decision rules, information, or all three.

II. Decision-Making Theory: From Rationality to the Garbage Can
    A. Increasing consistency in theory, increasing agreement on goals and decision rules, and improving quality of information will produce increasingly rational decisions in criminal justice.
    B. In an influential book, March and Simon (1958) first questioned the rationality of the decision-making process. They pointed out that decisions were made on the basis of bounded rationality, partly because decision makers are incapable of collecting and handling the kinds of information needed for completely rational decisions.
    C. The notion of bounded rationality seems to be especially appropriate for criminal justice decisions. Many decisions, especially those regarding offenders, are characterized by volumes of information about their history and background. It is important to recognize that the information is selectively collected and interpreted and that decision processes are influenced by the organizations of the criminal justice system.

D. Satisfycing, or the attainment of acceptable rather than optimal results, is also a useful concept in criminal justice.
E. Decision makers handle problems of ambiguity by developing sets of performance programs, or standardized methods of responding to problem. Organizations possess a repertoire of responses, or a <u>garbage can</u> of ready made answers.
F. Organization members modify their perceptions of problems to justify actions.
   1. The garbage can analogy has its appeal as a means of understanding some decision making in criminal justice.
G. Stability and routinization of decision making are products of bounded rationality.
H. Another important contribution of the concept of bounded rationality is recognition of the cognitive limitations of individual decision makers. Not only must decision makers deal with multiple goals and possibly conflicting theories, and not only are they controlled by organizational practices, but they can effectively handle only small quantities of information.

III. Organization Culture and Decision Making
   A. Satisfycing and garbage can decision making are both bounded by organizational culture.
   B. Organizational culture is defined as ready made answers to problems (Simon and March, 1958),or a set of basic assumptions and beliefs shared by organizational members that are taken for granted.
   C. The "decisions on who make decisions, when and how are based upon past practices, routine, and assumptions about who is best suited to make decisions and what information is considered reliable.

IV. Politics and Decision Making
   A. External politics consist of the influence that outside parties have on the organization's mission and the direction the organization takes.
   B. Internal politics are the influences caused by the number of conflicting individuals and groups.

V. Characteristics of Decision Makers
   A. Sequentialists - Decision makers who use their experience to determine what information are most important. They consider items in a sequential fashion.
   B. Ah Yes! Decision Maker - They collect large amounts of information and search for patterns in that information.
   C. The Simplifier - They reduce complex problems to their simplest form.
   D. Ratifiers - They wait for comments from others and agree with them.

VI. Characteristics of Information
    A. Accuracy, although needed, is difficult in criminal justice
        1. Much of the information needed in criminal justice decisions is collected from people who have an interest in the outcomes or the process.
        2. There is a need in criminal justice to use summary information which distorts accuracy. Criminal histories, personality assessments, and other records are examples of summaries.
    B. Another characteristic of information is the order in which it is presented. The first pieces of information are likely to be more influential than later pieces.
        1. Decision makers using sequential strategies become invested in their decisions and tend to devalue new information.

VII. Discretion
    A. The goals of decisions are general and complex and discretionary decisions are not completely unregulated. Three significant implications follow from this perspective.
        1. First, discretion can be viewed as necessary and useful.
        2. Second, the boundaries or regulations of discretionary decisions can be studied and understood.
        3. Because they can be understood they can be influenced without eliminating discretion.
    B. The recognition that discretionary decisions can be highly predictable also suggests methods of affecting those decisions.
    C. By structuring rather than eliminating discretion, this process recognizes that sentencing is a complex process in which judicial discretion is useful and beneficial.
        1. Instead of viewing discretionary decisions as unconstrained by law or policy, this approach is based on identifying and building on implicit constraints.
        2. The patterns of previous decisions reveal those constraints, and studying those patterns provides a productive method for influencing discretion while still noting its importance.

VIII. Prediction
    A. The prediction of human behavior is generally thought of as a highly rational scientific process.
        1. Even when nonexperts make predictive decisions, this lack of expertise is generally not viewed as detracting from the rationality of the process.
    B. Many criminal justice decision involve prediction of future behavior.

IX. Improving Criminal Justice Decisions
   A. Improvement in criminal justice decision making means making rational decisions. Although completely rational decision making may be an unattainable goal, the process can be moved in the direction of being more rational now that it is from an organizational perspective.
   B. Equity in criminal justice processing means that similar offenders in similar circumstances are treated in similar ways.
      1. Legal and ethical arguments support equity in decision making.
   C. A second theme is accuracy.
      1. It is obvious that we should strive to see that persons not guilty of crimes are not arrested and that those released on parole do not commit additional crimes.
      2. It is equally important to strive to see that guilty persons are subject to arrest and that those denied parole based on prediction would, in fact, fail.
   D. A third theme, is consistency with theory
      1. Decision makers should strive to articulate the theories that underlie their decisions and to make future decisions consistent with those theories.
      2. We must appreciate, however, that the theories may be inconsistent with concerns for equity and accuracy.
   E. A fourth theme of decision making in criminal justice is consistency with resources. While we strive for consistency with theory, we must also consider pragmatic interests.
   F. Finally, a fifth theme is that both the process and the outcome should help to improve decision making in the future. This theme implies a cybernetic approach to improving decisions. Decision making should be guided by continuing assessments of equity, accuracy, and consistency with theory and resources.
      1. Improving decision making is an ongoing, evolutionary process
   G. When possible, group rather than individual decisions should be encouraged.
      1. Groups tend to be more willing to take risks than individuals.
      2. Group decisions, then, lessen the conservative influences of minimax criteria.
      3. Group discussion about what information is considered relevant and how information is processed also encourages consistency in both the process and outcome of decisions.
   H. Decision makers should also be encouraged to frame their decisions as probability estimates for two reasons.
      1. The accuracy of those estimates can then be checked against actual behavior and policy can dictate the outcome of decisions when probability estimates are made explicit.

Exercise

Students: In your small groups answer the issues concerning the case. Consider the chapter objectives, key words and the outline.

Case Study Rational Sentencing: Whose Rationality?

Mary had worked as a probation officer for a little over a year. She had a degree in criminology and criminal justice and was excited about working in probation. After a few weeks of unprogrammed on the job training she was pleased that much of her university course work had given her some basis for the procedural aspect of the work. Mary especially felt that her college instructor, an ex-probation officer, had given her a fairly good grasp of the presentence investigation process (PSI). As a result, she was assigned her own PSI work more quickly than most novices. However, a novice she was and she hadn't been given many complex or perplexing cases. Her last PSI assignment was a bit more complex then most. She had been assigned a PSI on a sex offender, specifically statutory rape. A 22 year old male had a month long sexual relationship with a 16 year old girl. When her parents discovered the relationship, they filed charges over the objections of the girl. The defendant had an earlier arrest for disorderly conduct as a result of a fight in a local tavern, and a number of speeding tickets. He had worked steadily but had moved from job to job as an auto mechanic. He also admitted to being a recovering drug and alcohol addict. Mary verified his attendance in recovery treatment and tests showed that he was drug and alcohol free. The girl apparently had a difficult relationship with her parents, had dropped out of school, and was a drug and alcohol abuser. She convinced Mary during the PSI process that she was attempting to recover from her addiction and the defendant was the only person significant in her life who was supporting her attempt to recover. The girl also admitted to being sexually active and did not view her relationship with a 22 year old male as anyone's business.

Mary collected a great deal of additional information and considered her recommendation. She was in favor of granting the defendant probation on the condition he avoid contact with the 16 year old at least until she reached the age of majority. Mary also applied a statistical risk prediction model, which helped her conclude the defendant would not be a likely candidate for recidivism. She recommended probation with the condition the defendant would not have any contact with the girl until she turned 18 and presented her recommendation to her supervisor Brian.

Brian immediately said "Mary, we don't like to put sex offenders on probation. I don't like your recommendation." This is technically a sex offense," Mary answered, " but I don't see any evidence of the defendant digressing and getting involved with young girls as a pattern. I think he and the girl's mutual neuroses met which resulted in their relationship. I think it had more to do with the similar needs and personality disorder they both share."

"Cool", said Brian, "what if he meets a 14 year old who is a loser like him."

"Look Brian, I did a risk prediction on him and I really don't believe there is much of a chance of this repeating its if he keeps his interest in the victim, she will be an adult in about 18 months and the case is closed."

Brian closed the file and looked at her, "Mary, let me be honest with you. A month before you got here, we took a chance and put a child molester on probation. We did that because his parents had a team of lawyers and psychologists testify that he would be Ok and I suspect there some social links between the prosecutor, the judge, and the family of the creep, the family of the victim seemed charitable and felt the scum bag would benefit from psychiatric guidance. They didn't want to harm this asshole's life, the humiliation of being arrested was enough punishment. You know all the arguments. Well, the judge went against our unwritten policy and put him on probation. Guess what? He stacked his glove compartment back up with candy and was cruising the local elementary school a month after he was on probation. He snatched some kid into his car and fortunately was caught. Unfortunately, the press got hold of the whole thing and we took the heat."

"But it's not rational to compare that case with this one" Mary protested. "Its apples and oranges."

"Sure at its essence. But symbolically it's a sex offense and the press and all of the holier-than-thou groups are waiting for us to put a sex offender on probation. Believe me, the judge will not put this guy back on the street. Consider him a burnt of offering to the public for our last mistake."

"That's ugly," Mary declared. "I can't let this guy go to prison to satisfy some base political and vindictive needs of the public. The judge is supposed to have the courage to dispense justice, not satisfy the rabble."

"Easy Mary, that won't solve anything," Brian smiled. "Work out a compromise. Why don't you recommend jail time followed by some form of computer monitoring with probation?"

"Well, this disappoints me. But I guess you are saying if I recommend probation, he

is going to prison."
Brian stood up. The meeting was over. "That's right you're catching on now."

Case Study Questions

1. What role should political concerns have in decision making? In the case study,

should rational guidelines have more importance in the decision than potential political concerns?

2. What cultural aspects of the organization's decision making did Mary learn through this experience? In addition, what limitations are present within "rational" models of decision making?

3. In this case study, could cultural and political concerns be made part of the formal decision making processes? Can these cultural and political concerns be kept out of the decision making? Can prediction models address these concerns?

4. Design a process for sentencing, on a case by case basis how sex offenders should be sentencing according to the seriousness of the offense and the history of the offender.

Chapter 13
Organizational Effectiveness

Chapter Overview

For many people, the very concept of organization implies purpose, and the question of how well purposes are met is central to understanding organizations. Organizational effectiveness is thus a central theme in both the pragmatically oriented literature on management and the theoretically oriented literature of organizational behavior. For many managers, determining effectiveness involves identifying the criteria with which to assess effectiveness, measuring these criteria, and weighing the various outcomes. Implicit in these steps, however, are important theoretical questions such as: Effectiveness for whom? How are outcomes to be measured? What is a good outcome? Such inescapable questions illustrate the complexity of the concept of organizational effectiveness.

That complexity is evident in many discussions of organizations (see Peters and Waterman, 1982). For example, Tayloristic managers might cringe at a policy that Minnesota Mining & Manufacturing Co. (3M) finds central to its effectiveness. At 3M some employees are expected to steal company time and material for their own creative enterprises in the hopes that this theft will produce marketable innovations. Those sticky Post-It notes illustrate the potential for success in this approach. Managers at Ford also grappled with definitions of organizational effectiveness when, in the late 1970s, they allegedly used a cost-benefit analysis to decide not to recall Pintos, even though they knew the faulty gas tank design was linked to fires and the subsequent deaths of some of their customers (Cullen, Maflkestad, and Cavender, 1987).

In criminal justice the question of effectiveness is equally complicated. For example, what criteria for effectiveness should drive prison policies on overcrowding? In the mid-1980s, the Illinois Department of Corrections granted massive numbers of good-time deductions, thus permitting the early release of thousands of prisoners, before the courts intervened to stop the policy. Although the department argued that the policy was necessary for the effective management of the prison population, prosecutors argued that it violated correction's fundamental purpose of protecting the public from convicted criminals (Austin, 1986). The Florida Department of Corrections faced a similar situation when it retroactively rescinded good time credits for prisoners, thereby delaying the release of some offenders and reincarcerating others when it was found that they were let out too soon. Some offenders went to court, and the Supreme Court ruled that such a policy of rescinding good time credits was in violation of the Constitution's clause prohibiting, in effect, retroactive punishment. The result was the release of hundreds of felons, some of whom were serious offenders. Arguing from a public protection perspective, some politicians advocated that a constitutional amendment be passed to prevent the provision of good time credits to prisoners on the basis of advancing public protection as the primary purpose of criminal sentencing (CNN, 1997).

In this chapter we examine the questions posed by these examples. We begin by defining effectiveness and noting the political consequences of this definition. We then focus on theories of organizational effectiveness, paying special attention to the limitations of the models used frequently in organizational assessments. After examining a variety of methods for assessing effectiveness, the chapter ends with a discussion of key issues to consider in determining the effectiveness of criminal justice organizations.

Learning Objectives

When finished studying this chapter the reader will be able to:

1. Define and list the difficulties of The Goal Model.
2. List and briefly discuss the three significant elements of the Process Approach.
3. Define Organizational Effectiveness.
4. Briefly discuss the methods of assessing organizational effectiveness.
5. Define Variable Analysis.

Key Terms

Variable Analysis
Organizational Effectiveness
The Goal Model
Systems Perspective
Official Goals
Operative Goals
Counterparadigm

Congruence
Goal Consensus
Goal Optimization
Strategic-Constituency
Process approach
System Resource Model
Participant-Satisfaction

Chapter Outline

I. What Is Organizational Effectiveness?
    A. Effectiveness refers to the degree of congruence between organizational goals and some observed outcome.
        1. Some have argued that organizational survival is the best indicator of effectiveness.
        2. Others have focused on adaptability to the environment rather than simply on survival.
        3. Most scholars focusing on organizational goals have also argued that effectiveness is a multidimensional concept and have advocated the use of multiple measures to assess it.
    B. Cameron (1981) identifies three reasons why the concept of organizational effectiveness remains muddled.
        1. First, there are important differences in the way scholars have conceptualized organizations.
        2. A second but related reason for the confusion surrounding the concept of effectiveness is the complexity of organizations
        3. Third, the confusion has been enhanced by the fact that researchers have often used different, non-overlapping criteria, thus limiting the accumulation of empirical evidence about organizational effectiveness.
    C. Organizations can be effective or ineffective in a number of different ways, and these ways may be relatively independent of one another.
        1. The list includes productivity, efficiency, employee absenteeism, turnover, goal consensus, conflict, participation in decision making, stability, and communications.

II. Theories of Organizational Effectiveness
    A. The Goal Model
        1. The goal model is the most common theoretical perspective on effectiveness.
        2. It is both simple and complex. In its simplest form, the goal model defines effectiveness as the degree to which an organization realizes its goals (Etzioni, 1964).
        3. The model posits that organizations can be understood as rational entities.
        4. Evaluators assume that an organization's goals can be identified,
        5. Evaluators assume that organizations are motivated to meet those goals and progress toward them can be measured.
    B. Difficulties with Goal model.
        1. Most organizations have multiple and conflicting goals.
        2. Conflicting goals reflect conflicts absorbed by the organization

    from society at large.
  3. Public organizations are designed to be ineffective when effectiveness is ascertained by a broad based goal model.
  4. Official goals are generally for public consumption and can be found in annual reports and broad policy statements.
  5. Operative goals are generally derived from official goals but tell us exactly what the organization is trying to do.
  6. Another problem with focusing on organizational goals relates to the consequences of measuring goal attainment.
  7. Measuring goal attainment not only leaves some activity within an organization unrecognized but may narrow activity so that only those goals whose attainment is measured are met.
  8. A final concern about the goal model of effectiveness deals with the relationship between goal attainment and consequences for the organization. In public organizations this relationship is not at all straightforward. Lipsky (1980), for example, suggests that the demand for services in street-level bureaucracies will always increase to meet (or exceed) supply.
C. The goal model, then, is a complex framework in which to consider organizational effectiveness.
  1. Despite its limitations, however, the assessment of effectiveness continues to be largely a process of identifying goals, measuring them, and comparing the results against some standard.

III. The counterparadigm to the goal model (see Hall, 1982)
 A. Participant-satisfaction or strategic-constituency models.
   1. They view effective organizations as serving the interests of key constituencies, which may include resource providers, suppliers, users of an organization's products, or even clients in social service agencies.
   2. Effective organizations are able to maintain the contributions of these constituencies.
 B. Process approach.
   1. Under this model, effectiveness is described as a process rather than an end state, as might be the case under the goal model.
   2. The process approach consists of three related components:
    a. goal optimization,
    b. a systems perspective,
    c. and an emphasis on behavior within organizations.
   3. Goal optimization refers to the need to balance goals and thus to optimize multiple goals rather than achieve a particular one.
   4. A systems view incorporates concerns for changes in an

            organization's environment.
- 5. The behavioral emphasis suggests attention to the possible contributions of individual employees to organizational effectiveness.
- 6. The effective organization is one in which goals are responsive to the environment, optimization of multiple goals is pursued, and employees all contribute to meeting those goals.

C. System Resource Model.
- 1. Organizations are not assumed to possess goals, nor is goal accomplishment a relevant consideration. Instead, an organization is effective to the extent that it can obtain needed resources from its environment.

IV. Methods of Assessing Effectiveness
  A. Reviewing a variety of theoretical perspectives on effectiveness is useful because it not only points out the limitations of the goal model but also provides alternative ways of considering organizations.
  1. It is clear that the goal model dominates efforts to assess organizations.
  2. Studies based on this model involve the identification and measurement of some goal or goals.
  3. Variable Analysis - Sophisticated studies of this type try to examine causal links in the attainment of some goal. For example, they may examine the contribution of training or supervision style to job satisfaction.

V. Variable Analysis.
  A. Research designs that attempt to measure the attainment of some goal.
  1. In the assessment of organizational effectiveness, variable analysis refers to research designs in attempt to measure the attainment of some goal.
  2. Measurement of some outcome variable is often accompanied by investigation of the relationship between that outcome and independent variables.
  3. These studies, then, not only lead to general statements about effectiveness based on goal attainment but also provide information on what may contribute to effectiveness and thus on how effectiveness may be enhanced.
  4. Variable analysis is the most common approach to studying effectiveness in criminal justice.

Exercise

Students: In your small groups answer the issues concerning the questions. Consider the chapter objectives, key words and the outline. The questions are in the Chapter 13 for discussion section.

1. Local jails are complex organizations. Consider how you might assess the effectiveness of your own local jail. What internal and external constituencies exist How might their views of effectiveness differ from that of the jail administration?

2. Describe the goals of your local police department. How do official and operative goals compare? What variables would you suggest using to measure achievement of those goals? Is the meaning of the variables clear?

Chapter 14
Change and Innovation

Chapter Overview

This chapter focuses on organizational change within the criminal justice system and its agencies. Organizational change and the concepts and theories surrounding change can apply to minor procedural changes within an agency or to sweeping reforms that change the philosophy and operations of an entire system. At one extreme, changes can take place in an agency because of decisions on the part of agency members. At the other extreme, major, system wide change is typically the result of reform movements that emanate from cohesive groups within society or the polity in its entirety. Historically, such organizational change takes place within the context of general social changes that create, or are created by, different perspectives, ideas, or paradigms. For example, the criminal justice work force is rapidly becoming more diverse with the inclusion of minorities and women. This change, which itself will impact the system, has its roots in the earlier civil rights movement that, in turn produced legislation assuring minorities and women an equal right to employment opportunities, which, again, led to affirmative action requirements and programs. Rothman (1980) argues that the prison reforms that took place at the beginning of the century were the natural consequence of the "progressive era," during which all social institutions were being questioned and changed. The perceived need for reform and change in the criminal justice system preceded the progressive era however. Attempts to bring reform to the criminal justice system began at least as early as the mid-1800s. Prison reform was pursued in New York and Pennsylvania. In essence, our present parole system, which is being challenged and has been eliminated in some states, was developed in the late 1800s to emulate the "successful" system of penology developed by Sir Walter Croften in Ireland (Barnes and Teeters, 1959). In 1870, penologists from across the United States met in Cincinnati at the National Congress of Penitentiary and Reformatory Discipline. The goal of the dedicated members of the Congress was to reform and reorganize the existing American penal system. In 1931, the National Commission on Law Observance and Enforcement published the fourteen-volume Wickersham Commission Report, which provided recommendations to improve our criminal justice systems' ability to manage crime and delinquency.

In 1973 massive volumes of recommendations to improve police, courts, corrections, and the juvenile justice system were written by the National Advisory Commission on Criminal Justice Standards and Goals. The commission was provided with $1.75 million through the Law Enforcement Assistance Administration (LEAA), which was created in the 1960s to respond to increasing crime, civil and racial disturbances, and looting during riots. The unrest, both civil and political, shed doubt on the ability of criminal justice institutions to impose law and order, rehabilitate and control offenders, and in general impose social control in an efficient and just manner. Change and innovation were seen as desperately needed throughout the system. Millions of dollars in grants were provided to state and local criminal justice agencies through LEAA to assist them in making their operations effective and efficient and in the hope that the standards and goals promulgated by the National Advisory Commission would be implemented.

Today, the effectiveness and practices of the criminal justice system are continually being challenged by society or the political and legal system. Massive overcrowding of prisons and jails and the apparent influx of mentally ill offenders into our correctional institutions are stretching the ability of our corrections system to perform basic tasks. Police agencies are being restructured through the implementation of foot-patrol units or team policing. The practice of indeterminate sentencing and parole has been challenged by both liberal and conservative members of the police (Cullen and Gilbert, 1982); and traditional judicial sentencing practices are being challenged. The perceived need for reform within the criminal justice system is ever present, and both substantive and symbolic changes have been made to meet that need. In the long term, change has been a part of the criminal justice system and will continue to take place in the future. Change is inevitable and leads to progress. The change manifested in simple agency alterations or in major reforms may be purposive or crescive (Warren, 1977). Crescive change is inadvertent or unplanned and is independent of an organization's control. Crescive change may come about in spite of organizational efforts at self-direction. It can result from environmental influences on an organization or from internal organizational conflict (see chapters 3 and 10 on organizational environments and conflict). Purposive change results from conscious, deliberate, and planned efforts by organizational members, typically managers. Purposive change may be a response to changing environmental conditions or pressures, to internal conflict, or to organizational members' perceived needs to change or improve aspects of their system. Crescive and purposive change are obviously not mutually exclusive processes. Purposive change represents an "intervention into a flow of events that will in any case result in change.... Consequently, the decision is not whether or not there will be change, but rather what one's part will be in shaping or channeling inexorable change" (Warren, 1977: 10). In this chapter, we will be concerned primarily with purposive, or planned, change as it applies to the agencies of the criminal justice system. Change may be required or can take place at every level of an organization and in every nook and cranny. An organization may change its mission and social function or may continuously change procedures. It is beyond the scope of this chapter to consider every possible change within an organization. Throughout, we discuss organizational change as a general phenomenon rather than attempt to apply the concept of change to every facet of a criminal justice agency or system.

Learning Objectives

When finished studying this chapter the reader will be able to:

1. Define why change occurs.
2. List and briefly discuss four significant elements of a planned change.
3. Define Organizational Effectiveness .
4. Briefly discuss the seven characteristics of organizations that readily facilitate change.
5. Describe the processes to overcoming resistance to change.

Key Terms

Unfreezing
Changing
Organizational Sources
Refreezing
Performance Gap
Organizational Development

Forecasting
Resistance To Change
Personal Sources
Innovations
Climate
planned Change

Chapter Outline

I. Why Change Occurs
   A. Change will occur as a result of pressures from an agency's environment or from conflict within the agency.
      1. The agency may enter into deliberate or planned change efforts.
      2. Organizational executives must first perceive a need for change, that "something is broke and needs to be fixed."
      3. A performance gap may be recognized by agency executives, personnel, clients, or other constituencies (Downs, 1967).
      4. An agency official will not generally search for alternative policies or methods unless a performance gap is made apparent.
   B. A performance gap may be produced by any of four major events:
      1. Employee turnover
      2. Internal structural or technical changes
      3. External or environmental changes
      4. Repercussions of an agency's performance
   C. Organizational change can be understood as a bridge that links an organization with its environment.
      1. Organizations modify their internal workings to adapt to external environmental pressures and constraints.
      2. The adaptation process is a form of purposive change in response to a perceived performance gap.

II. The Process of Organizational Change
   A. Planned Change
      1. The optimal approach to creating substantial change in an agency is to enter into a deliberate and rational process of planned change.
      2. Planned change requires that decision makers make rational decisions
      3. They must possess all pertinent information and must not be constrained by time or other resource limitations in the planning and decision-making process.
      4. Decision makers at best operate under "bounded rationality" where they have limited knowledge and a finite amount of time and resources to dedicate to the decision-making process.
      5. An extension of the concept of bounded rationality is the garbage-can theory, which suggests that organizational change is typically less than a deliberate, rational process.
   B. The garbage-can theory posits a model of organizations in which problems become receptacles for people to toss in solutions that interest them.

1. Agency decision makers have favorite solutions stored away that are searching for problems (Perrow, 1986).
2. The "can" becomes an opportunity for agency members or decision makers to put forward their particular solution, which can include their own agendas.

C. Planned change requires innovation and accepts problems as opportunities to pursue real improvement in an agency's performance.
1. Planned change requires first over coming organizational decision making routines such as "garbage can" solutions, seeking knee jerk quick fixes, confusing symptoms with problems, over concern for protecting boundaries, use of least cost solutions and methods to placate external pressures.
2. Planned change also requires a view to the future rather than merely adapting to immediate pressures and problems. Leadership and vision are required to overcome these bad organizational habits that quietly subvert planned change.

D. Planned change requires an ongoing and substantive commitment for the long-run health of an organization.
1. The process of planned change demands routine and continuous examination of an agency's operations as well as the expectations and demands of the agency's clients and constituents to discover existing and potential problems that will create performance gaps.

III. Planning in Criminal Justice
A. Planning can be thought of as the systematic application of the concept of planned change.
1. Planning is a process that precedes decision making, that gives explicit consideration to the future, and that seeks coordination among sets of interrelated decisions or actions.
2. Planning ideally allows the achievement of ends and the making of rational choices among alternative programs.

B. The planning process is the first step in developing and implementing planned change.
1. The tasks of planners are identifying agency goals and problems, forecasting, and generating and testing alternatives.
2. In planning and decision making, it is important to consistently review the basic purposes of the agency as rational planning requires a clear understanding of mission or goals as well as the values implicit in the agency's purpose.
3. The identification of problems is crucial to planning and to avoiding the garbage-can approach to management. Planners and

managers who perceive a performance gap need to analyze the root causes of the gap or problem.
4. Forecasting is obviously an important aspect of planning, especially long-term planning.
   a. Forecasting requires that planners and decision makers attempt to project into the future to understand prospective problems and to estimate the impact decisions will have on the agency or its constituents.
5. Generating and selecting appropriate alternative solutions to problems is another crucial step in planning. Planners must construct a series of possible alternative solutions for the problems that have been identified.

C. Planning in general, as we have described it here, is, at best, difficult and bounded by constraints.
   1. Purely rational planning may be especially difficult for criminal justice agencies.
   2. Rational planning requires that an agency's goals are congruent rather than contradictory, that the goals are clear and known to the agency members or decision makers, and that means-ends relationships are understood (Hudzik and Cordner, 1983).

D. The planning process has the potential of clarifying goals or at least prioritizing agency objectives.

IV. Resistance to Change
   A. Planning is the technical aspect of planned change. Implementing change is the human and more difficult aspect of planned change.
      1. The human side requires that agency members change their work behaviors and possibly their values, depending on the breadth or depth of the prescribed change.
      2. A natural resistance to change exists in almost all organizations.
      3. Obstacles and sources of resistance to change must be identified and eliminated or controlled if planned change is to be successful.
      4. If obstacles to change are beyond the control of an agency or its planners, plans may have to be tailored within those constraints.
   B. Personal Sources
      1. Personal resistance is especially apparent in areas where community policing or foot patrol is being implemented. Community police who walk the beat are viewed by other officers as "social workers" who are "not real cops" (Trojanowicz and Carter, 1988).

2. The role of the community police officer is viewed by many traditional police officers and administrators as being in conflict with their traditional role.

C. Organizational Sources
1. An agency's traditional practices, values, structure, or leadership can influence the success or failure of attempts to implement change.
2. Resistance to change due to organizational climate and sunk costs in past decisions and routines is common.
3. Organizations with rigid structures are typically those with well-established traditions, belief systems, routines, and practices, as well as little history of change.
4. Also, large, powerful organizations that are capable of influencing their environments will typically place more effort into resisting change than into conforming to pressures for change.

D. Organizations that readily facilitate change have several characteristics in common. In addition to having a history of change, (Burnes and Stalker, 1961; Hage and Aiken, 1977) found that change-ready organizations share the following characteristics:
1. High complexity in terms of professional training.
2. High decentralization of power.
3. Low formalization.
4. Low stratification in terms of differential distribution of rewards.
5. Low emphasis on volume (as opposed to quality) of production.
6. Low emphasis on efficiency in terms of cost or service.
7. High level of job satisfaction on the part of organizational members.

E. In addition, organizational change requires, in essence, that the organization's routines be altered.
1. Routines develop in all organizations that survive for an extended period of time. Routines provide certainty and purpose to organizational members.
2. An organization, and its members, will face uncertainty with the elimination of well-established routines and therefore will resist their elimination.
3. More specifically, many criminal justice routines are imposed by statute and case law, and subroutines are created within the organization to establish conformity or the appearance of conformity to prevailing laws.

F. Large police agencies and correctional systems are organized along bureaucratic lines and are often considered to be paramilitary organizations.
1. They have a clear chain of command and a hierarchy of authority supported with formal rules and regulations. The rigid formality

of such agencies requires and creates a set of routines that are often seen as a statement of organizational purpose and that are difficult to eliminate or alter.
G. Resistance to change is also a function of the magnitude and depth of the change that is being proposed.
   1. Fundamental change therefore encounters a great deal more resistance than attempts to create circumstantial or procedural change.
H. Organizations whose members are unionized face another potentially powerful constraint on change.
   1. Management-labor contracts often call for specific behavior on the part of both management and labor. These agreements reinforce particular routines and make them unalterable for the duration of the contract.
I. Successful innovation within an organization is dependent, in part, on the positive association between external pressures for change and internally perceived need for change (Griener, 1967).
   1. In other words, when an agency's constituents and members both perceive a performance gap, the momentum for a change will be strengthened by the congruent pressures.
   2. Public support is, therefore, important to effect planned change.

V. Characteristics of Innovations
   A. The first set of characteristics relates to the social and economic cost and cost effectiveness of innovation and change. Innovations with a higher price tag will be entered into with greater reluctance.
      1. If the innovation will create a high return on the initial investment or will improve an agency's efficiency, the innovation will be more attractive than one that does not.
   B. The extent to which organizational change creates risk or uncertainty will also affect the likelihood of innovation.
      1. Innovations that are compatible with the existing organizational structure and are not complex will pose less risk and uncertainty to an agency than those that are incompatible and complex.
      2. Change that is reversible creates less apprehension and has less potential for causing risk and uncertainty.
   C. Plans for innovations that emanate within organizations and are timely have a better opportunity for acceptance than externally imposed or poorly timed innovations because internal innovations have greater credibility.
      1. Timeliness suggests that innovative ideas are put forward to meet a need at a moment when consensus about the problem and its

source exists among organizational members.
2. Timely ideas have a stronger chance of survival in an organization than ideas that must be sold to or forced on agency members.
D. The larger the mass of people involved in the change process, the more implementation will be impeded.
1. If innovation is likely to affect the general public or external groups, more individuals will be involved in the process of change than if these groups are not affected.

VI. Overcoming Resistance to Change
   A. Change ultimately requires unfreezing, changing, and refreezing the behavior of an organization's members (Lewin, 1958). This process requires a set of strategies to overcome resistance to change.
      1. The responsibility for overcoming resistance to change within an agency typically falls on change agents-usually management (Bennis, 1966).
      2. The extent to which managers have a commitment to change and are capable of overcoming change-resistant staff is an important determinant of successful implementation of planned change (Bennis, 1966; Zaltman, Duncan, and Holbeck' 1973; Skolnick and Rayley, 1986).
      3. Strategies for change can be aimed at the individuals in an agency, the agency's structure and system, or the organizational climate (the interpersonal style of relationships) or at combinations of these targets (Huse, 1975; Steers, 1977).
   B. Individual Change Strategies
      1. The assumption underlying this approach is that individuals or groups of individuals within an agency must modify their attitudes, skills, and behaviors.
   C. Structural and Systems Change Strategies
      1. Realizing improved methods may require a rearrangement of an organization's policies, procedures, and reward-punishment system.
      2. Major modifications may be required in the basic structure of the organization as opposed to simply altering the work behaviors of the members.
      3. Before workers' behaviors can change, basic structural aspects of the system that constrain their behaviors must be changed.
   D. Organizational-Climate Change Strategies
      1. The assumption behind attacking organizational climate to initiate change is that the behaviors in an organization are largely a product of the organization's culture (Schein, 1985).
      2. The routines of an organization and the work behaviors of its

members are constrained by the collective value structure of the organization and the emotional and social interaction among its members.

3. An organizational climate may further be described as having the following dimensions (Steers, 1977):

   a. Task structure - The degree to which the methods used to accomplish tasks are spelled out by an organization.

   b. Reward-punishment relationship - The degree to which the granting of additional rewards such as promotions and salary increases is based on performance and merit instead of other considerations like seniority.

   c. Decision centralization - The extent to which important decisions are reserved for top management.

   d. Achievement emphasis - The desire on the part of the people in an organization to do a good job and contribute to the performance objectives of the organization.

   e. Training and development emphasis - The degree to which an organization tries to support the performance of individuals through appropriate training and development experiences.

   f. Security versus risk - The degree to which pressures in an organization lead to feelings of insecurity and anxiety on the part of its members.

   g. Openness versus defensiveness - The degree to which people try to cover their mistakes and look good rather than communicate freely and cooperate.

   h. Status and morale - The general feeling among individuals that the organization is a good place in which to work.

   i. Recognition and feedback - The degree to which employees know what their supervisors and management think of their work and the degree to which management supports employees.

   j. General organizational competence and flexibility - The degree to which an organization knows what its goals are and pursues them in a flexible and innovative manner. Includes the extent to which it anticipates problems, develops new methods, and develops new skills in people before problems become crises.

4. The task at hand, therefore, is to create a climate within the organization that facilitates change in its culture and simultaneously affects traditional agency practices and habits to allow changes in the values, attitudes, and persona

interactions of its members. For example, if organizational members tend to be defensive and insecure, they will be reluctant to venture into new roles, even if they are prescribed by management.
5. If communication is poor or decision making is centralized, it will be difficult to gain the active participation of organizational members in the change process (Duffee, 1986).
6. Creating an organizational climate that is conducive to cooperative change can be an overwhelming task, especially if the change is prompted by extreme conflict within an agency. However, any change within an agency that goes beyond the alteration of simple procedures or change that is consensual will probably face impediments from within the environmental and cultural aspects of the system.
   a. Therefore, steps for dealing with an agency's climate should be considered in the early phases of planned change.

VII. Organizational Development
   A. Organizational development (OD) focuses on the environmental influences of an organization.
      1. The process attempts to alter values, routines, and structures of a system simultaneously in an attempt to create an atmosphere in which obstacles to change can be identified and minimized (French, 1969).
      2. Traditionally, OD programs have been the responsibility of a change agent, an individual whose sole role is to promote change within a system.
         a. The change agent may come from within an agency-usually from management-or may be a consultant from outside the agency.
   B. These are some of the objectives of OD programs (French, 1969:24):
      1. To increase the level of trust and support among members,
      2. To increase the incidence of confronting problems,
      3. To create an environment where authority is based on expertise as well as being assigned,
      4. To increase the level of personal satisfaction among organizational members
      5. To increase open communication within the organization.
   C. As a field of social and management science, OD relies on a multidisciplinary approach and draws heavily on psychology, sociology, and anthropology as well as on information from motivation, personality, and learning theory, and on research on group dynamics, leadership, power, and organizational behavior.

D. The techniques used in OD are based, in part-upon Theory Y assumptions that individuals are responsible and can be motivated most readily when they are given responsibility.
   1. Hence the techniques are aimed at getting organizational members' active contribution in identifying agency problems and developing solutions rather than leaving that task to a few of the management elite.
E. OD techniques and programs include survey feedback, which is a pencil-and-paper method of gathering information from agency members, and team building, which allows agency members to form groups that do not conform to traditional social or authority-oriented patterns.
F. Team building creates fresh subsets of interpersonal communications among agency members and overcomes traditional barriers to communication.
G. Training, such as sensitivity training, that focuses on agency members values, perceptions of agency problems, and commitments to agency goals is a common OD technique.
   1. Training of this nature facilitates information gathering, open communication, and examination of personal objectives within the framework of role objectives and organizational objectives.
H. Such techniques and programs attempt to get organizational members actively involved in the change process while providing them with an opportunity for open dialogue across ranks to improve communication, examine problems and solutions, and identify impediments to change.
I. OD requires active participation of organizational members in the process of management and especially change.
   1. Criminal justice agencies are typically bureaucratic, paramilitary organizations, in which communications flow predominantly downward. Upward communication, while theoretically possible, is severely limited.
   2. Lateral communication is contrary to organizational structure and practices.
J. The preponderance of traditional routines precludes the quality and quantity of member participation in organizational decision making that is requisite to the practice of OD.
   1. Utilizing change agent outside consultants or internal specialists-on an ad hoc basis when change seems to be inevitable will have limited value.

VIII. Unintended Consequences of Change
   A. The final outcomes of a change effort may be different from those desired by change agents or planners.
      1. Social interventions fail as policy makers and planners fall into regressive traps for several reasons.
      2. The multiplicity and priority of goals of target groups may not be understood thoroughly if they are understood at all.
      3. Goals may be displaced by the bureaucratic emphasis on process rather than outcome.
   B. Program evaluation needs may also pervert the desired ends as agencies may evaluate outcomes of the program that are readily measurable or show favorable results rather than the original ends of a program.
   C. The successful change agent needs to be free of traditional organizational paradigms to posses the vision to look for future contingencies.
   D. The visionary leader needs to have an understanding of the within his or her own organization that limit vision.

IX. Implications for Criminal Justice Managers
   A. Managers seek stability, order and certainty.
      1. Planning and budgeting are completed with a context for stability and control.
      2. Managers and administrators also police the organization's boundaries to keep out disruptive influences and to provide the organization with stability.
      3. By virtue of their tasks, their view is narrow and planning serves to solve problems that threaten stability.
   B. Developing new paradigms requires recognizing and setting aside the assumptions that dominate the organization.
   C. The importance of leadership and a holistic approach is demonstrated by the following mode of change in a police department:
      1. Influencing younger members, then promoting them to positions of influence,
      2. Urging retirement of older officers and replacing them with new officers who can be successfully indoctrinated,
      3. Identifying and enlisting older officers who will buy into new ideas,
      4. Training middle managers through the chiefs office to ensure proper indoctrination,
      5. Sending trained middle managers into the field in leadership positions to indoctrinate other members of the organization,
      6. Applying the coercive power of the chiefs office to punish those fighting change.

Exercise

Students: In your small groups answer the issues concerning the case. Consider the chapter objectives, key words and the outline.

You have been hired by the Sheriff's Department as an organizational development consultant to resolve the issues dividing the department. The Undersheriff met with you and requested the following tasks in an effort to meet the objectives of the attempted organizational change:

1. Evaluate jack's strategy for implementing the community policing approach. What has he done correctly and what should he do now?

2. Identify the primary resistances to the change.

3. Develop a strategy for implementing the community policing change from this point on.

Case Study - Adobe Sheriff's Department Patrol Division

The patrol captain, Jack Jenson, was just hired by the undersheriff from outside the department for the purpose of up-grading the law enforcement operations. Specifically, Jack and the undersheriff have agreed that a community policing approach would be best for the department and that innovation would require a revamp of patrol policies and generally upgrading the training and overall caliber of patrol people.

Presently, the patrol division has a reduced staff because of newer officers quitting. The existing patrol captain was fired because he could not or would not implement progressive changes. The officers remaining were very loyal to the old captain. The undersheriff decided not to promote anyone for the past year because he knew a change was coming. The morale of the division is very low because of the popular captain being fired, because of the lack of supervision and because of the anticipated changes.

The detective captain, Dirk Hotshot, and his division seem to have some special status in the department. While the undersheriff manages the department's operations, the detective captain spends much time with the sheriff and together they make decisions that effect the detectives. In fact, the sheriff, when he is around, works with the detectives on exciting or interesting cases but usually ignores the other divisions of the department.

The jail division captain, Martha Harried, is not very progressive and does not know about community policing. She is a former patrol Lt. but has not paid much attention to the other divisions of the department because of jail operations changes forced by new constitutional requirements. Morale in the jail is not very good and the quality of staff and supervisors is average.

The administration captain, Snidely Whiplash, is responsible for the budget, CiVil section, records and training. He is a former patrol captain who is very conservative philosophically and an authoritarian as a manager. He strongly opposes the community policing concept.

The first week on the job Jack implemented the following;

> 1. He met with all staff and informed them that there was going to be a major change in patrol philosophy and he explained the concepts of community policing.
>
> 2. He stated in the meeting that the three vacant supervisor positions would be filled by persons who were skilled in community problem solving and who had supervisor skills that fit the requirements of managing community officers who will have more freedom on the street. The promotions would come from within the department or from outside the department depending on the qualifications of the applicants.
>
> 3. He designed a training program with the training officer to be implemented immediately as soon as new staff were hired.
>
> 4. He established that new supervisors, along with extensive police experience, would have degrees in management or strong experience supervising high level employees and that new officers would have 4 year college degrees.
>
> 5. He met with the local newspaper and with community service groups to explain the concepts of community policing and to inform them of the patrol division's new direction.

Within the first month, Jack discovered that; first, the training officer had done nothing to develop the training program. When confronted the trainer stated that he did not think it was important because the department would probably not implement community policing and that his captain told him it was not a high priority.

Second, six patrol officers were outwardly mocking and talking against the community policing idea. When confronted by Jack they stated that, generally, detectives and jail staff were telling them that the concept would never work or have the whole support of the sheriff's department.

Third, the status of the patrol budget was unclear and Jack could not get a straight answer from Snidely concerning the amounts in patrol budget categories.

Fourth, Dirk and Martha were constantly complaining that the patrol division was getting all new and higher level staff and they had problems that were more important that required immediate attention. They were vocal about how officers with college degrees would upset the department.

Fifth, the sheriff, while basking in the positive public attention that Jack's community meetings generated, did not become involved in the department's conflicts.

The undersheriff was continually supportive of Jack but he also did nothing to resolve conflicts.

Chapter 15
Research in Criminal Justice Organizations

Chapter Overview

Unanimous agreement exists that the justice system ought to be efficient, effective and fair. Less accord, however, exists about how best to secure these essential qualities or how to measure whether they have been achieved. Unlike marks on a ruler, criminal justice measures are not neutral standards but are factors that enter into the process being analyzed identifying relative degrees of improvement in fairness in sentencing, for example, would still indicate that the sentencing process was giving weight to information not legally relevant (Greenfeld, 1993).

To today's students of management in criminal justice, the 1967 President's Commission on Law Enforcement and the Administration of Justice may seem to deserve little more than an historical footnote. But the commission's contributions to contemporary criminal justice have been far greater than that would suggest. And its aspirations and expectations for what the field would be like as we approach the year 2000 were even more grand. Not only did the commission emphasize the idea that criminal justice could best be thought of as a system rather than disconnected agencies and organizations, but the vision was one of system governed by a process of rational planning. Although the Commission found there was little empirical research to guide its recommendations at the time, research was to play a central role in the future. In the Commissions vision, empirical research would provide a powerful force for change in the field of criminal justice.

The power of research also had many other champions which could be expected to influence the management of criminal justice. From Frederick Taylor, who sought statistical definitions of a good day's work, through Kurt Lewin, whose action research model was driven by the dictum "Research that produces nothing but books will not suffice" (1947), generations of management models in business and industry have regarded the collection and analysis of data as critical. In today's widespread quality movement in industry, research plays a central role in the management process.

In this chapter we will examine the role of research in criminal justice organizations. We begin by considering the impact of social science research of the kind envisioned by the President's Commission. We will then look further at the nature of research in the organizational context and consider such varied types as basic research, applied research, evaluation research and action research.

Learning Objectives

When finished studying this chapter the reader will be able to:

1. Define Knowledge Utilization.
2. List and briefly discuss five significant elements contributing to problems in the research-practice relationship.
3. Define Knowledge as Power.
4. Describe the processes of power-coercive strategies
5. Describe the processes of normative-reeducative strategies.

Key Terms

The National Institute of Justice
The National Institute of Corrections
The National Council on Crime and Delinquency
In-House Research
Normative-reeducative Strategies
Action Research
Power-coercive Strategies

Chapter Outline

I. "Knowledge for what?
   A. In a classic work in 1939, Robert Lynd asked the question, "Knowledge for What?" and considered the role of social sciences in American Culture. The debate over the appropriate relationship between social science research and public policy continues today.
   B. The primary purpose of applied research is to develop knowledge that is directly useful to practitioners.
   C. Managers and ultimately front line workers must appreciate the value of research and social scientists must be able to respond to the needs of practitioners. They argue that working together emphasizes both process and product and is most likely to produce useful knowledge.
   D. For many researchers, criminal justice is an applied field in which studies

should be designed in a way to influence practice.
E. The National Institute of Justice (NIJ), the agency which funds that majority of government supported research on crime and criminal justice, has begun emphasizing the importance of partnerships between academics and criminal justice agencies.

II. Criminal Justice Organizations and Knowledge Utilization
A. Studies have also shown that organizational structure and management influence the use of research in organizations.

III. The Researcher and Knowledge Utilization
A. There is also another side to understanding the utilization of research in public policy. While we have considered organizational impediments to the use of research, researchers can also contribute to problems in the research-practice relationship.
1. Many practitioners may never be exposed to the available research.
2. The most important source of information for managers appeared to be the word of trusted colleagues or staff members.
3. The common method of dissemination of the results of social science research in criminal justice and other fields.
4. The writing style and narrow dissemination of academic research have been identified as major reasons some administrators report that research findings are of little use in their decisionmaking process.
5. Decision makers in organizations may have little time or ability to directly digest research findings but may instead rely on people with whom they have direct relationships.
B. The National Institute of Corrections has successfully used academics and practitioners in providing technical assistance for prisons and jails.
C. The National Council on Crime and Delinquency (NCCD) has also formed effective relationships between researchers and practitioners as states have struggled with how to project prison population growth and address crowding.

IV. In-House Research
A. In-house research, not to be contrasted with out-house research, refers to the development of the capacity within organizations to address the data and research needs of those organizations. That is often done

through separate units or research offices within the organizations.
- B. There is great potential for in house research efforts to overcome some of the problems discussed above. In house research units can establish credibility and gain the support of managers to overcome organizational resistance to research and research units can integrate researchers into the fabric of organizations thus overcoming the limitations associated with outside researchers and the research process.
- C. The potential strength of in-house research is found in the potential for close partnerships between managers and researchers.

V. Knowledge as Power
- A. The power of knowledge may contribute to rational processes within organizations; processes that can promote or resist change based on empirical evidence.
- B. That power may also be used in change strategies that Chin and Benne have described as power-coercive strategies. Under these strategies research is a source of coercive power.

VI. Knowledge as Understanding
- A. Chin and Benne describe a category of change strategies they call normative-reeducative strategies. These emphasize that understanding is a transactional process in which information is taken in, interpreted and acted upon according to the values and experiences of the consumer. The impetus for change comes not from the expert's analysis but rather from collaboration and experienced based learning.
- B. To describe normative reeducative strategies that are based in the collection and analysis of data, Kurt Lewin coined the term "action research."
    1. Lewin stressed the need for strengthening the relationships between research, training and action.
    2. He emphasized the need for collaborative relationships in organizations in which managers, workers and researchers came together to understand the need for change, to develop the knowledge base necessary to bring about change and monitor the process of change.

Exercise

Students: Form the class into small groups (3-6 persons per group) and resolve the following questions. Allow 30 - 45 minutes for preparation to report out findings. As the groups report consider discussions that relate to the chapter objectives, key words and the outline.

Discussion Questions

1. How do you think research has influenced the criminal justice system since the President's Commission in 1967. What examples can you give of research findings which have had a direct or indirect bearing on practice in the field?

2. Critique the major sources of data about crime in the United States. What are their strengths and weaknesses? How should they be used in research and how should that research influence management and policy. What cautions would you suggest?

3. How has research been used in your own experience studying criminal justice? In your education, has research generally been viewed as offering facts and truth? Have you seen examples in political campaigns or other circumstances where research has been used a source of coercive power? Have any of your assignments reflected a participatory or self-study approach? If not, what would such assignments look like?

4. Follow your local paper or talk with criminal justice officials in your community to identify a problem area facing criminal justice. Now design a research project to address it. In fact, design three: one reflecting a rational empirical approach, one based on power-coercive uses of data and one based on the normative re-educative self-study methods. Which strategy do you think would be most effective and why?

Correctional Leadership

•

Appendix A

Correctional Leadership:
Styles, Range And Appropriateness

Albert E. Roark, Paul L. Katsampes, Myrna Radl, and Paul A. Hansen

Instructions: This questionnaire was developed by criminal justice practitioners during training sessions at the National Academy of Corrections and it has been tested for its validity. The situations, the scoring, and the theory have been patterned after Hersey and Blanchard's Situational Leadership Instrument. These authors based their efforts on the Contingency Management Theory which is described in Chapter 7.

- The situations and possible answers are designed so that there is a best answer for each situation, a second best answer, a poor answer, and a very poor answer.

- The students should answer the situations individually and they should try to select the correct answer based on their knowledge now that they have completed the first two sections of the text.

- Allow approximately 20-30 minutes for students to complete the instrument. The process of administering the instrument and the following discussion may consume two or more hours.

- Score the instrument by circling the answers chosen in both columns of letters. Count the number of answers in each column. Enter column totals into the style range boxes by transferring column l totals to style l box, column 2 totals to style 2 box, column 3 totals to style 3 box, and column 4 totals to style 4 box.

- The situations are equally divided so that there are six best Directive answers, six best Coaching answers, six best Supportive answers, and six best Delegating answers. A page of the questionnaire instructions describes these leadership and decision making styles.

- The questionnaire scores will reveal the students' tendency to prefer one style over another and which styles they do not prefer. Review the styles and relate to the theory for the discussion concerning individual preferences and the groups preferences.

DESCRIPTION OF FOUR LEADERSHIP STYLES

1. Directing

A. *High task-centered and low relationship-centered leadership styles*
- The leader defines his/her subordinate's roles, work procedures, and deadlines.
- Communication is mostly one-way, downward from the leader to the subordinates.
- The leader makes all work unit decisions with little or no input from the subordinates.
- The leader personally inspects all work unit activities.

2. Coaching

A high task-centered and high relationship-centered leadership style
- The leader, with some input from subordinates, defines in/her subordinate's roles, work procedures, and deadlines.
- Communication is somewhat two-way, downward from the leader to the subordinates and occasionally upward from the subordinates to the leader.
- The leader asks for subordinate input into work unit decisions, but reserves the right to make the final choice.

3. Supporting

A low task-centered and high relationship-centered leadership style
- The leader and subordinates together define the subordinate's roles, work procedures, and deadlines.
- Communication is mostly two-way; downward from the leader to the subordinates, upward from the subordinates to the leader.
- The leader and the subordinates share equally in making work unit decisions.
- The leader only becomes involved in work unit activities in exceptional situations.

4. Delegating

A low task-centered and low relationship-centered leadership style
- The leader delegates the responsibility of defining the subordinate's roles, work procedures, and deadlines to the subordinate.
- Communication between leader and subordinates is limited.
- The leader delegates work unit decisions to the subordinates.
- The leader only becomes involved in work unit activities in exceptional situations.

Style Range and Appropriateness

	Columns (1)	(2)	(3)	(4)	Best Answers
1	A	C	E	B	A
2	D	A	C	B	A
3	C	A	D	B	D
4	B	D	A	C	C
5	C	B	D	A	C
6	B	D	A	C	D
7	A	C	B	D	B
8	C	B	D	A	A
9	C	B	D	A	C
10	B	D	A	C	D
11	A	C	B	D	B
12	C	A	D	B	B
13	A	C	B	D	A
14	D	A	C	B	A
15	C	A	D	B	D
16	B	D	A	C	C
17	C	B	D	A	C
18	B	D	A	C	D
19	A	C	B	D	B
20	C	B	D	A	A
21	C	B	D	A	C
22	B	D	A	C	D
23	A	C	B	D	B
24	<u>C</u>	<u>A</u>	<u>D</u>	<u>B</u>	<u>B</u>

Totals

Place your answers in the appropriate box under the style that matches the answer column. There should be six answers in each box if the participant chose every correct best answer. The box with the highest score will indicate your leadership style preference.

STYLE 3	STYLE 2
High Relationship - Low Task Participating/Supporting	High Relationship - High Task Coaching/Consulting

STYLE 4	STYLE 1
Low Relationship - Low Task Delegating	Low Relationship - High Task Directing

Correctional Leadership Questionnaire

1. Your corrections officers are not responding to your suggestions and concerns for their safety regarding Performance in searching inmates after visitation. Increasing amounts of contraband have been found in cells, The policy is written and clear on the matter.

   A. Insist on the use of proper procedures of searching inmates after visitation for security.
   B. Allow subordinates to define problems and set goals for ensuring that proper procedures are followed for ensuring security. But don't gush.
   C. Call staff meeting to reaffirm policies and procedures and engage in group problem solving.
   D. Let the group work out their problems.

2. All inspections reflect that the effectiveness of the floor officers is improving. You have been making sure that officers were aware of their responsibilities to perform up to standards. But you have started asking them for input on the Job.

   A. Tell them they are doing a good Job end to keep up the good work, while still emphasizing the importance of standards.
   B. Do nothing in particular.
   C. Congratulate them on their improvement and emphasize their personal importance.
   D. Maintain emphasis on officer's responsibilities to perform up to standard.

3. Inmate living quarters are dirty and unkempt. A previous manager established a once a week inspection by himself held every Friday. You have delegated your supervisors to implement a plan whereby their subordinates are to conduct daily cleanliness inspections. Your supervisors communicate well and normally are very efficient in carrying out this type of delegated task. Obviously, the plan is not working.

   A. Call a meeting and work with the supervisor to collectively figure out a way to get it done.
   B. Advise the supervisors you haven't noticed any improvement and take no further action.
   C. Advise the supervisors the plan is not working and tell them how to get it done.
   D. Stress the importance of the cleanliness issue and tell them of your confidence in their ability to get it resolved and support their efforts.

4. A change is needed in the recreation schedule you make available to your inmates. Staff members have offered suggestions which could be beneficial. Your past experience with this group has proved their efficiency.

    A. Call a staff meeting. Give the staff your ideas, allow them input In the final decision and then allow them to implement the changes.
    B. Put out a memo, state your change; supervise closely to see that the change is done properly.
    C. Let staff handle it.
    D. Listen to their recommendations but implement your change.

5. Certain members of the staff have been reporting late for their shift. This problem has reached such a degree that the other staff members are complaining. They have been continually reminded to report for work on time.

    A. Intentionally, do not intervene. They will work it out.
    B. Work with the staff and together engage in problem solving.
    C. Redefine rules and regulations, and supervise carefully.
    D. Encourage group to work on problem and be supportive of their efforts.

6. All inspections reflect that the effectiveness of the officers is improving. You have been making sure that they were aware of their responsibilities.

    A. Congratulate them on their improvement.
    B. Maintain emphasis on officers' responsibilities.
    C. Take no definite action.
    D. Tell them they are doing a good job while emphasizing the importance of their responsibilities.

7. You are moving into a new correctional facility. Your correctional staff will be transferred to the new facility. This staff has demonstrated good management and they have made suggestions for operational changes and procedures.

    A. Write revised procedures and supervise carefully.
    B. Get involved with corrections staff in developing change in policy and allow staff to organize the implementation.
    C. Accept the input, but maintain directions of overall policies.
    D. Do not get involved. Transfer and operate as before.

8. You have recently been assigned as a new administrator. It is an efficient facility and the corrections officers are communicating well, work hard, and are knowledgeable. Because of shortages in manpower, you must change some job assignments and the watch schedule.

   A. Inform them of the desired change and date to be completed and allow them to work it out.
   B. Involve all staff members in the job assignment and scheduling, assisting them in the change.
   C. Take charge and tell them what you have changed and how you want the changes implemented.
   D. Involve all staff members in the Job assignment changes and watch scheduling, and have them work out the details.

9. Your property room personnel are not operating according to rules and regulations; this is resulting in lost property, poor control of inmates' commissary, and an inordinate amount of attention to staff by supervisors.

   A. Avoid confrontation. Leave things alone.
   B. Discuss property room performance with the group and then you decide what changes will be made.
   C. Emphasize the use of uniform procedures and the necessity for task accomplishment.
   D. Allow property room personnel to discuss the situation and don't push for changes.

10. The medical forms have been revised to meet standards. The subordinates are not carrying out the implementation of the more complex medical form. They usually carry out responsibilities effectively.

    A. Allow group to revise form within guidelines to their liking without supervision.
    B. Implement and redefine new form. Supervise carefully.
    C. Allow situation to continue as is. Do not interfere.
    D. Incorporate subordinates' recommendations in the revision, but maintain standards control.

11. You need new policy and procedures in your organization. Your line supervisors have drafted them before and have done well with them. They communicate with each other and work well as a team, usually getting all group tasks accomplished the way you want. On this occasion you delegated this task again but results are less than your expectations.

A. Call a group meeting and tell them you are unhappy with their performance and tell them how you want the task done.
B. Tell the line supervisors that they have performed well in the past and, as this is a very important task, you have confidence in their ability to complete the job.
C. Have a meeting of all line supervisors and ask them to figure out a way to complete the task with your help.
D. Tell the line supervisors that the task needs to be done end then leave them alone.

12. You are replacing a supervisor who has retired. Although morale Is marginal, the group's performance has continued to be good. They take responsibility, make good plans, and anticipate future needs.

    A. Discuss the current situation with subordinates and determine what changes are needed.
    B. Avoid intervention; take no immediate action.
    C. Establish new policies and procedures and see that they are adhered to.
    D. Involve subordinates In planning and reinforce their good performance.

13. Your dietician/cook, though highly qualified and experienced, has of late not met standards. Her performance in the past has been questionable. An outside circumstance is suspected of causing the problem.
    A. Emphasize the necessity of meeting standards.
    B. Remind her of your open door policy to discuss the problem.
    C. Talk to her and discuss the problem. Then decide what to do.
    D.   Wait and see what happens.

14. Roger's performance in handling inmates is improving. He has been taking training sessions on the supervision of inmates.
    A. You personally make him aware of his improvements but continue to stress responsibilities.
    B. Take no action.
    C. Tell Roger that he did a real good Job.
    D. Give Roger more training and continue to stress responsibilities and expected standards.

15. You have a highly qualified Sergeant transferred to your shift. Previous performance indicates he completes assigned tasks with little or no direct supervision.
   A. Tell him he has been doing a good Job for previous supervisors and discuss with him how you and he will operate together in the future.
   B. Welcome him aboard and tell him to keep up the good work.
   C. Review policy and procedures with him and explain in detail what you expect from him.
   D. Involve the Sergeant in decision making and reinforce good contributions.

16. A Sergeant has made a recommendation for duty changes. The Sergeant has been instrumental in making previous productive recommendations and assisting in implementing changes. You are considering making these duty changes.

   A. Encourage the Sergeant In his development, organization, and implementation of the duty changes, but don't be too directive.
   B. Define the duty changes and supervise carefully.
   C. Allow the Sergeant to organize and implement the changes needed.
   D. Compliment the Sergeant on recommended changes but maintain control of implementation.

17. The Admissions Department of your facility has been changed to a separate section with its own supervisor. This change has resulted in strong resistance and deteriorating performance and, as the commander, you must resolve It.
   A. Charge the group to formulate the procedure needed and bring It back to you for review.
   B. Review charge with group and explain the relative value. Take recommendations for possible changes, but maintain control.
   C. Redefine the policy for the group and closely supervise its implementation.
   D. Allow the group to participate in a review of the policy and consider possible revisions.

18. The shift commander has accepted a new position. She ran an efficient, tightly controlled operation. You, as the new commander, want to maintain a well-run operation but would like to begin humanizing the work environment for the staff.

   A. Do what you can to make staff feel important and involved.
   B. Emphasize compliance with the policy and procedure manual.
   C. Let staff continue as is and do not intervene.
   D. Get staff involved in decision making, but ensure that objectives are met.

19. A 65-year-old supervisor has been with the agency for 5 years. He previously spent 37 years with the federal penal system. This person is superlative In inmate control and total prison security! However, he is weak on documentation and supervision.
   A. Act immediately, telling the supervisor to start doing his total Job, or you'll replace him.
   B. Encourage the supervisor to assume his full responsibilities and duties, and be supportive of him.
   C. Talk with the supervisor and get his interaction, but emphasize that he must carry out his responsibilities and meet the standards.
   D. Allow the supervisor to function as he is presently.

20. A new procedure has been created for the movement of inmates to and from the recreation area. The Line Sergeant assigned to the post has developed a count procedure for that post that deviates somewhat from the normal, but for the past two weeks has proved to be 100% accurate. He suggests that you implement his procedure as formal policy.
   A. Allow the Sergeant to submit his procedure for implementation.
   B. Evaluate the procedure for two more weeks and submit same for mutual evaluation.
   C. Inform the Sergeant the final decision for implementation of procedure is yours.
   D. Compliment the sergeant for his valuable input.

21. The new senior officer on the shift is the observer of a supervisor who refuses to take the required responsibility of the shift. The result is that various assignments are not being met because the Junior officers do not have the experience to complete the tasks.
   A. Don't interfere. The senior officer will handle it.
   B. Discuss the problem with the officer and out if there may be a better way of resolving the situation. Then you decide what should be done.
   C. Advise the senior officer as per department policy if a supervisor performs unsatisfactorily. The senior officer must assume all responsibility of that shift, and, if he fails to do so, disciplinary actions will be taken against him.
   D. Explain why the senior officer must assume the responsibility. Stress the senior cfficer's ability and fine record.

22. A manager has just returned from a training program where he learned numerous new policies and procedures he feels must be implemented. He summons his administrator, Ms. Seete, who is very capable of understanding and implementing directions and who has an excellent work record. Then he:

   A. Congratulates the administrator on her good past performance, asks for her opinion of the new policies, and begins implementation.
   B. Emphasizes the necessity for the changes to be made immediately.
   C. Asks her to review and implement the new procedures as she sees f~t.
   D. Asks her input about implementing them but retains responsibility for implementation. Together they make plans.

23. A line supervisor Sergeant who is a shift commander is experiencing difficulty with an officer on the shift who he believes is not adequately performing his duties. The Sergeant is a good supervisor with a good record.

   A. Transfer the officer to another shift.
   B. Hold an interview with the Sergeant to convey your confidence in him.
   C. Discuss the officer performance with the Sergeant and instruct him to confront the officer involved.
   D. Allow the Sergeant to resolve his problems.

24. You, the administrator, have a supervisor on the day shift who has been with the department for is years. He has held the position of Lieutenant (Shift supervisor) for the past 15 years. During this entire period he has been an exemplary employee and an excellent leader. During the past week he has been late on two occasions. His being late hasn't affected his performance or the performance of his team in any visible way.

   A. Engage in friendly interaction, but continue to make sure that he is aware of his responsibilities and expected standards of performance.
   B. Leave the employee alone.
   C. Redefine his roles and responsibilities and supervise carefully.
   D. Call him into your office for an informal conversation about possible problems he may be having.

Team Project

•

Appendix B

Team Project

- The team project materials consist of the following:
    1. A <u>team project summary face sheet</u> showing the agency to be analyzed and a list of the team members
    2. A <u>team effectiveness chart</u> matrix showing the score of six criteria as a result of group meeting processes.
    3. An <u>action agenda</u> form that shows the <u>project timetable</u> and the group's tasks and assignments.
    4. An <u>organizational analysis questionnaire</u> that includes questions and alternative answers that reflect the six box model.
    5. A <u>group life cycle chart</u> that shows the potential development of groups that progress toward interdependence and positive problem solving.
    6. A <u>group roles chart</u> that shows positive and negative roles group members might assume during the problem solving process.

The purpose of the group project is to learn how to work as a team solving organizational problems. The team members must learn how to plan the project, make assignments according to individual strengths, and to organize and develop a report as a joint effort.

The result of the team project is to complete an organizational analysis using the six box model (a analysis approach designed by Marvin R. Weisbord, Organizational Diagnosis: A Workbook of Theory and Practice, Addison-Wesley Publishing Company, Reading, Massachusetts, 1989). The elements of the "six box model" represent an encompassing of organizational processes. Each element or "box" includes analysis of the formal system and the informal system. The descriptions make up the diagnosis target areas. The following are the elements of the <u>Organizational Diagnosis</u>:

Purpose

- The purpose of the organization is its mission, goals and objectives. The purpose should be clear to all employees and, even if they don't agreed or if they have different philosophies from the organization, they should be working towards the stated mission.

- Organizations need to continually check their environment and their functioning to assess whether or not their purposes still are relevant.

- The important questions include; is our goal relevant?; are our goals clear? and is there agreement among workers concerning our goals?

Structure

- The structure of an organization is a picture of the levels of authority and the formal relationships between functioning groups.

- The structure must be an accurate picture of legitimate authority and it should be a formal method for facilitating work and the accomplishment of the organization's goals.

Relationships

- Relationships involve people, groups, technology and other functional elements working together successfully.

- The salient diagnosis point is assessing how conflict in the organization is handled. Conflict is inevitable but the manner it is dealt with results in either a positive or growth outcome or a negative outcome.

Rewards

- The reward system, formal and informal, needs to be analyzed. The important data to be collected involves how people are motivated to complete the work, what behavior they feel rewarded for and do the rewards relate to accomplishing the organizational goals.

- The reward system may be in place but there may not be a "fit" between the manager's perception of the system's effectiveness and the needs of the individual workers.

- The rewards need to be assessed for their fairness among workers. The equality between employees is critical to perceived benefits and treatment by management.

Leadership

- Managers use the resources of personnel and materials to accomplish organizational goals. Their methods include facilitating the coordination of the elements of the organization to create a product.

- The manager's methods include leadership style, focusing on tasks and relationships, identifying purposes, managing conflict and maintaining accountability.

- The measure of a manger's effectiveness is the amount of influence or power employees perceive the manager to have or allow the manager to have.

Helpful Mechanisms

• Helpful Mechanisms are the customized vehicles assisting people to cooperate or to coordinate activities. Examples are policy and procedure manuals, meetings, memos, reports or positions that exist for linking organizational elements.

• Helpful mechanisms need to be assessed for their effectiveness and worth.

Organizational Diagnosis Elements[1]

Elements	Formal System	Informal System
1. Purposes	Goal Clarity	Goal Agreement
2. Structure	Functional	How work is actually done or not done
3. Relationships	Who should cooperate whom on what Which technologies should be used for	How effective is coordination Quality of relationships Conflict management
4. Rewards	Formal Reward System	Informal Reward System
5. Leadership	What do top people manage What systems are in use	What are actual norms and behaviors of the management system
6. Helpful Mechanisms	Policy Manuals Management Information System	What are systems actually used for and are they subverted

---

[1] This chart was derived in part from Marvin R. Weisbord's "Six Box Model"

Organizational Diagnosis Questionnaire

The purpose of this questionnaire is to identify organizational problems and conflict in an effort to resolve issues in a positive and healthy manner, assisting the organization accomplishing its objectives and making it a better place to work.

Action Research Model
- Data Collection - Organize the facts and opinions concerning how the organization is working. (consultant)
- Diagnosis - Identify the "gaps" between what is and what ought to be as supported by the data. (consultant with management team)
- Action - Develop and implement strategies to solve the problems and conflicts. (management team)
- Evaluation - How did we do? What are new "gaps" or problems? (management team)

Important: The information offered in the questionnaire and through interviews to the consultant is confidential. No names are required on documents. The consultant will summarize the information for presentation to the management staff.

Purpose

Attached is the mission statement of the_____ .
Please read it and comment by answering the following questions;

1. Does the behavior of management through supervision decisions and policies support the principles of this mission?
    1. Never
    2. Sometimes
    3. Usually
    4. Always

2. Considering professional standards, public opinion and offender needs, how appropriate is the mission?
    1. Not appropriate
    2. Somewhat appropriate
    3. Mostly appropriate
    4. Very appropriate

3. To what extent are workers in the organization committed to the mission?
    1. Not at all
    2. Somewhat
    3. Usually
    4. Always

4. How clear are the goals of the organization to the workers?
    1. Not at all
    2. Somewhat
    3. Usually
    4. Always

Structure

5. Are the levels of authority (supervision) clear and do people operate through normal channels?

    1. Structure is <u>not clear and people do not get things done</u> because of this problem
    2. Structure is <u>not clear and people get things done through informal</u> channels
    3. Structure is <u>clear but people get things done through informal</u> channels
    4. Structure is <u>clear and people get things done through formal</u> channels

6. Do supervisors have enough authority to make decisions concerning work at their assigned level?

    1. No authority
    2. Some authority
    3. Usually have authority
    4. Authority is very clear

Helpful Mechanisms

Please measure the effectiveness of the following helpful mechanisms in assisting workers get the job accomplished;

7. Policy and Procedure Manual
    1. Not at all   2. Sometimes   3. Usually   4. Always

8. Shift Change Meetings
    1. Not at all   2. Sometimes   3. Usually   4. Always

9. Memos
    1. Not at all   2. Sometimes   3. Usually   4. Always

10. Other Meetings
    1. Not at all   2. Sometimes   3. Usually   4. Always

Relationships

- The following descriptions are ways to solve organizational conflicts. Please rank order how your organization attempts to solve its problems.

A. Forcing - More powerful people get their way
B. Smoothing - People either pretend that there are no differences or minimize their importance
C. Avoiding - It's disloyal to raise disagreements openly
D. Bargaining - People negotiate, holding some cards in the hole, playing for their own maximum advantage
E. Confronting - An effort is made to surface differences, examine disagreements and to initiate problem solving

    11. Most Often Used   _____

    12. Second Most Often Used   _____

    13. Least Method Used   _____

- List the three most serious conflicts in the Organization that are presently not resolved;

14. _____

15. _____

16. _____

Rewards

17. Do workers in the organization feel motivated to perform productively?
    1. Not at all   2. Sometimes   3. Usually   4. Always

18. Are behaviors that support the organizational goals rewarded?
    1. Not at all   2. Sometimes   3. Usually   4. Always

19. Does the Organization encourage responsibility and achievement?
    1. Not at all   2. Sometimes   3. Usually   4. Always

20. Is advancement based on productivity?
    1. Not at all   2. Sometimes   3. Usually   4. Always

21. Are there positive supervisor-employee relations?
    1. Not at all   2. Sometimes   3. Usually   4. Always

22. Are supervisors technically competent?
    1. Not at all   2. Sometimes   3. Usually   4. Always

23. Are organization policies clear?
    1. Not at all   2. Sometimes   3. Usually   4. Always

24. Are the working conditions adequate?
    1. Not at all   2. Sometimes   3. Usually   4. Always

25. Are the salaries adequate?
    1. Not at all   2. Sometimes   3. Usually   4. Always

Leadership

- The following descriptions are categories of leadership style. Please classify the levels of supervision using these descriptions.

    1. Directs - Tells employees what to do; watches the workers closely.
    2. Consults - Asks employees for ideas and opinions but reserves the final decisions for themselves.
    3. Participates - Makes decisions with employees as a team.
    4. Delegates - Delegates responsibility to employees, allowing workers to make important decisions.

and

- For the following list place the appropriate number for how much influence each manager has with you.

1- no influence   2- a little influence   3- much influence   4- Very much influence

	Style	Influence
26. Top Manager	_____	_____
27. Your Division Manager	_____	_____
28. Your Immediate Supervisor	_____	_____

Team Project Summary

Team
Name_____

Project
Organization_____

    Agency Contact Person_____

    Address_____

    Phone Number_____

Team Members (Print names and phone numbers)

1.

2.

3.

4.

5.

6

7.

8.

Group_____ Date _____ Meeting #_____

Team Meeting Effectiveness

Complete the team effectiveness chart and describe the group process for each team meeting. The chart should first be scored by each individual and then the scores averaged for the team meeting chart. The meeting notes should be complied by one person as a representative of the group. The notes should reflect the attendance, the productivity of the group during this meeting and the failures or conflicts addressed.

Team Effectiveness Chart

10						
9						
8						
7						
6						
5						
4						
3						
2						
1						
↕ Score Criteria ↦	Using Strengths of Individuals	Confronting Conflicts	Creativity	Making Clear Decisions	Staying on the Timetable	Constructive Participation

Meeting Notes....................

Appendix B - 9

Team Project Timetable and Action Agenda

Project

Task	Person Assigned	Date to be Completed	Resources Needed

Group Life Cycles

Group Development	Interpersonal Issues
<u>Dependence</u> - group forms orientation and introductions, working on membership	<u>Inclusion</u> - superficial, polite, confusion
<u>Counter Dependence</u> - group storms, power, decision making process, attacks on leader	<u>Control</u> - establishing operating rules. emotional response to task demands
<u>Independence</u> - group develops norms and functional relationships, workers assume responsibility for tasks	<u>Affection</u> - individuals are able to negotiate honestly, they begin to like each other
Collaboration · **Synergy** · Working Together · High Productivity Inter-dependence	√

Group Roles

Task	Process
1. Initiator - proposes tasks, goals, actions, suggests a procedure	**1. Harmonizer** - attempts to reconcile conflicts, reduces tension, getting people to explore differences.
2. Informer - offers ideas, facts and opinions	**2. Gatekeeper** - facilitates the participation of others, helps to keep communication channels open.
3. Clarifier - defines terms, clarifies issues	**3. Consensus Tester** - asks the group for individual decisions, tests for a possible conclusion.
4. Summarizer - pulls related ideas together, restates suggestions, offers a decision or conclusion for the group to consider.	**4. Encourager** - indicates to others by facial expression or remarks of acceptance of others ideas.
5. Reality Tester - makes a critical analysis of ideas, tests the ideas to see if they would work.	**5. Compromiser** - modifys position in interest of group cohesion.

Blocking Roles

1. **Aggressor** - *deflating others' status, attacking the group or its values, joking in a passive aggressive manner.*

2. **Blocker** - *disagreeing and opposing beyond reason, resisting for personally oriented reasons, using hidden agenda to block group's progress.*

3. **Dominator** - *asserts superiority to control or manipulate the group.*

4. **Playboy or Girl** - *jokes around beyond reducing conflict to avoid responsibility of group process.*

5. **Avoidance Behavior** - *stays off task subject to avoid responsibility or commitment, prevents group from facing up to controversy.*

Test Bank

•

Appendix C

Chapter 1
Basic Concepts for Understanding Criminal Justice Organizations

1. _____ are a significant part of our lives.
    a. Agencies
    b. Organizations
    c. Government
    d. Bureaucracies

2. The _____, _____, and _____ of individual organizations differs.
    a. size, structure and purpose
    b. labor, action and hierarchy
    c. rules, regulations, and policies
    d. environment, atmosphere and personnel

3. Organizations require some _____ and structure.
    a. goal
    b. mission
    c. boundary
    d. action

4. One of the definitions of organizations for Klofas, Stojkovic and Kalinich.
    a. The activities of organizations are related to some complex set of goals.
    b. Organizations are limited to rigid forms.
    c. Organizations are consciously coordinated activities or forces of two or more persons.
    d. All organizations are bureaucracies.

5. Management is a process involving elements of a _____.
    a. team
    b. group
    c. organization
    d. goal

6. The "closed system" view is unresponsive to their _____.
    a. team
    b. organization
    c. group
    d. environment

7. The "_____-_____" view was developed by Katz and Kahn.
    a. closed system
    b. open system

Appendix C - 1

c. input system
d. output system

8. The bottom line on the open-systems view is that it allows us to take into account how _____ influence their environment as well as how they are influenced by it.
    a. groups
    b. activities
    c. management
    d. organizations

9. The organizations of the criminal justice system have multiple and _____ goals.
    a. conflicting
    b. quality
    c. complex
    d. adaptable

10. The way organizations are evaluated is also influenced by the _____ .
    a. agency
    b. environment
    c. system
    d. goals

11. The internal constituencies are: clients, _____, legal and budgetary considerations and workforce in general in criminal justice.
    a. environments
    b. groups
    c. supervisors
    d. employees

12. The "Pareto Solution" is one which seeks maximal_____ attainment.
    a. goal
    b. skill
    c. concept
    d. conflict

13. _____organizations reflect conflict from the environment.
    a. Private
    b. Profit
    c. Non-profit
    d. Public

14. The major criticism of the closed-system view is that it is too _____.

a. rigid
   b. complex
   c. simplistic
   d. confusing

15. _____ is a process.
    a. Supervision
    b. Authority
    c. Management
    d. Membership

16. Clear division of labor was a structural concept developed by _____.
    a. Klofas
    b. Weber
    c. Kalinich
    d. Stojkovic

17. Barnard developed the idea that _____ consciously coordinate activities or forces of two or more persons.
    a. structures
    b. bureaucracies
    c. organizations
    d. groups

18. _____ is a function which may not be the sole responsibility of any particular office.
    a. Management
    b. Supervision
    c. Authority
    d. Communication

19. The _____ _____ staff determines organizational policy through application of discretion.
    a. first line
    b. front line
    c. middle line
    d. bottom line

20. Management is directed at the attainment of organizational _____.
    a. groups
    b. teams
    c. communication
    d. goals

Chapter 2
Structure of Criminal Justice Organizations

1. Which is not a description of the Federal Bureau of Prisons?
    a. Includes six metropolitan correctional centers (jails).
    b. Massive organization.
    c. Provides only minimum security.
    d. Provides maximum, medium and minimum security.

2. A chain of command with authority and responsibility being delegated from a central authority downward implies that the hierarchical system is a(an)_____.
    a. agency
    b. organization
    c. bureaucracy
    d. condition

3. Which of the following statements would not be true of a hierarchical structure?
    a. Expertise and knowledge reside at the top.
    b. Tasks are not specialized.
    c. Superior-subordinate relationships exist among personnel.
    d. Management styles are directed toward command and obedience.

4. Tasks can be taken on by groups and ____ sharing expertise in an open system.
    a. individuals
    b. players
    c. teams
    d. supervisors

5. ____specialization is dividing the work process into a number of smaller tasks.
    a. Control   b. Formal   c. Task   d. Risk

6. Decision making is decentralized if routinely made at the "_____" level.
    a. grass roots
    b. lower
    c. higher
    d. intermediate

7. _____the mission can provide organizational members and constituents a clear understanding of agencies purpose, goals and objectives.
    a. Ideally
    b. Ironically
    c. Visibly
    d. Appropriately

8. Comprehensive understanding of _____ through some form of training and education can be achieved by all staff.
   a. rules and regulations
   b. policies and procedures
   c. values and beliefs
   d. verbal and written rules

9. Hierarchy of positions, with graduation of _____ and privileges is a universal accompaniment of all complex organizations.
   a. honors
   b. awards
   c. pride
   d. contributors

10. Communication through chain of command can be _____.
    a. vertical or horizontal
    b. formal and informal
    c. inefficient and ineffective
    d. flat or tall

11. _____ and regulations are often considered as policy and procedures.
    a. command
    b. issues
    c. communication
    d. rules

12. All _____ have a mission.
    a. Organization   b. leaders   c. Bureaucracies   d. agencies

13. Organizations tend to _____ tasks and create a number of sub units.
    a. develop
    b. specialize
    c. activate
    d. originate

14. _____ who rely solely on the tools of the formal structure to control inmate political power will ultimately be rendered ineffective.
    a. Subordinates
    b. Supervisors
    c. Managers
    d. Administrators

15. The following describes a_____frame "...organizations are cultures that are propelled more by rituals, ceremonies, stories, heroes and myths than by rules or managerial authority..."
    a. symbolic
    b. structural
    c. human resource
    d. ritual

16. As seen on television, the "war" on crime and on drugs is an example of evoking symbols that cast the tasks/roles of actors as_____.
    a. rich and famous
    b. poor and helpless
    c. dramatic, heroic, dangerous and important
    d. arrogant, abusive and without worth

17. It was in the early _____when rehabilitation as a symbolic statement representing the role of correctional institutions lost its effectiveness.
    a. 1970s
    b. 1930s
    c. 1990s
    d. 1950s

18. In a formal structure,_____attempt to alter the script of what is being played out in the organization.
    a. managers
    b. subordinates
    c. line staff
    d. leaders

19. Who developed the formal and informal states of organizations?
    a. Barnard
    b. Downs
    c. Richmond
    d. Maslow

20. Meaningful participation by subordinates is the essence of_____.
    a. empowerment
    b. motivation
    c. control
    d. Apathy

Chapter 3
The Criminal Justice System In Its Environment

1. The _____ influences the substance and form of organizations.
    a. force
    b. environment
    c. focus
    d. mission

2. In general the environment is any phenomenon, event, group, individual, or system _____ to the organization.
    a. internal
    b. direct
    c. external
    d. indirect

3. There are direct and indirect effects of _____ in the environmental dimension.
    a. technology
    b. demographic
    c. ecological
    d. cultural

4. _____ and court decisions provide authority for criminal justice agencies.
    a. Rules
    b. Authority
    c. Legislation
    d. Constituents

5. Political conditions of an environment can impact upon an organization directly through pressures from _____ and _____.
    a. constituents and clients
    b. legislation and courts
    c. economics and demographics
    d. collectives and members

6. There are limitations on the number and scope of agencies which are directly influenced by _____ resource availability to public bureaucracies.
    a. political
    b. demographic
    c. cultural
    d. financial

7. Factors such as age, sex, race, ethnicity, and the population of a community all have an impact on the_____dimension.
   a. economic
   b. social
   c. political
   d. Demographic

8. The_____ dimension refers to components of the environment such as climate, geographic location, type of economy, and so on.
   a. political
   b. economic
   c. ecological
   d. cultural

9. The_____ dimension is defined as the collective norms, values, symbols, behaviors, and expectations of the members of a given society.
   a. Culture
   b. Ecological
   c. Political
   d. Legal

10. The_____system is also a part of the formal political system.
    a. law
    b. legal
    c. court
    d. justice

11. The external task environment of the criminal justice system are forces in the environment that are related directly to the goal setting and_____activities of the agency.
    a. political bodies
    b. criminal offenders
    c. social service
    d. goal directed

12. Task environments attempt to override the_____ goals.
    a. negotiated   b. official   c. agency   d. personnel

13. The environmental dimensions can range from simple to complex and from __
    a. static to dynamic
    b. input to output
    c. direct to indirect
    d. formal to informal

14. The ultimate goal of the criminal justice administrator is to simplify aspects of the _____ dynamic environment.
    a. simple
    b. homogeneous
    c. complex
    d. dominant

15. The _____ coalition is concerned with broad political and public opinion.
    a. dominant
    b. clientele
    c. environmental
    d decoupled

16. Work processors deal directly with _____.
    a. environments
    b. clientele
    c. authority
    d. boundaries

17. Organizations are _____-_____ and are dependent upon and constrained by environmental systems.
    a. closed-systems
    b. simple-systems
    c. complex-systems
    d. open-systems

18. Many organizations attempt to function in a _____-_____ orientation.
    a. open-systems
    b closed-systems
    c. complex-systems
    d. simple-systems

19. The role of the _____ administrator is to enter exchange relationships.
    a. jail
    b. police
    c. agency
    d. corporate

20. _____ management becomes an art.
    a. Private
    b. Public
    c. Corporate
    d. Middle

Appendix C - 9

Chapter 4
Problems of Communication

1. In interpersonal communication a _____ is one individual sending a message to another.
    a. supervisor
    b. dyed
    c. pathway
    d. FAX machine

2. Which one of the following is not a major barrier to communication?
    a. poor organizational climate
    b. preconceived ideas
    c. non-credibility of the source
    d. good communication skills

3. A traditional chain of command provides for a_____ set of communication paths.
    a. clear
    b. complex
    c. connived
    d. commercial

4. Which of the following is not true about upward communication?
    a. primary source of feedback for managers
    b. always sufficient to carry all messages
    c. lets lower level share information with managers
    d. can encourage employee participation

5. Every organization has a set of _____ for communication.
    a. games
    b. telephones
    c. rules
    d. company cars

6. Networks purposefully developed by management are considered_____.
    a. formal.
    b. rigid.
    c. informal.
    d. infamous.

7. Which of the following is an example of nonverbal communication?
   a. news releases
   b. TV ads
   c. lectures
   d. capital punishment

8. In the field of communication, load refers to_____.
   a. the pieces of information.
   b. rate and complexity.
   c. number of judgments.
   d. weight.

9. Assuring the distribution of_____ is, in part, the rationale for training.
   a. distributed information
   b. absolute information
   c. policy and procedures manuals
   d. department schedules

10. Motivational communications tell about_____.
    a. organizational or personal goals and values.
    b. consequences.
    c. the environment
    d. how to reach a goal.

11. Subsets of networks are always _____.
    a. mutually exclusive.
    b. formal.
    c. informal.
    d. overlapping.

12. The check and balance system in criminal justice tends to:
    a. create communication barriers.
    b. establish mutual priorities.
    c. enhance agreement among agencies.
    d. increase funding.

13. Who developed the idea of Exchange Theory?
    a. Maslow
    b. Mongue
    c. Marsden
    d. Marx

14. The glue that links exchange systems together is _____.
    a. motivation.
    b. communication.
    c. interpretation.
    d. information.

15. Linking pins are persons who _____.
    a. belong to two or more groups.
    b. run bowling alleys.
    c. are formal coordinators.
    d. work to defeat the exchange system.

16. What is one of the major problems in police-media communication?
    a. lax animal-control laws
    b. preconceived notions
    c. political support
    d. vigilante groups

17. An approach that encourages teamwork among agency staff is called _____.
    a. Generation X.
    b. First Amendment Right.
    c. Melancon.
    d. Theory Z.

18. There is a link between communication and_____in human services.
    a. efficiency
    b. directives
    c. programs
    d. routine tasks

19. Upgrading staff computer skills is a/an _____.
    a. assurance of effective communication.
    b. cost-effective program.
    c. lower order need in agency communications.
    d. necessary solution to communication problems.

20. The criminal justice system is run as a(an) _____ system.
    a. democratic
    b. authoritarian
    c. lateral
    d. underhanded

Chapter 5
Motivation of Personnel

1. The psychological definition of motivation depends on the _____ between the employee and the work environment.
    a. workman's compensation
    b. psychological contract
    c. application for employment
    d. learned values.

2. Needs theory is based on the work of _____.
    a. Martin
    b. Schein
    d. Freud
    c. Maslow

3. _____ is a critical factor in need orientation, according to some researchers.
    a. Good looks
    b. Money
    c. Age
    d. Sex appeal

4. If individuals could be matched to clearly identifiable tasks in corrections organizations, _____ could be enhanced.
    a. efficiency and effectiveness
    b. cultural diversity
    c. morale
    d. increased pay

5. In "The Human Side of Enterprise", who describes Theory X and Theory Y?
    a. Ideus
    b. Bennett
    c. Roberg
    d. McGregor

6. One of the following is not an ancillary belief of Theory X:
    a. individuals are self-centered.
    b. individuals are ambitious.
    c. individuals are not intelligent.
    d. individuals are resistant to change.

7. Theory Y assumes that
    a. people are resistant to organizational needs.
    b. people resist responsibility.
    c. people have potential for development.
    d. management should direct all goals of the organization.

8. McClelland originally developed the _____ theory of motivation.
    a. achievement
    b. power
    c. status
    d. behavior

9. What is a power motive that is impersonal?
    a. adversarial
    b. competitive
    c. simplistic
    d. socialized

10. The concept that performance equals motivation times ability is _____.
    a. irrational.
    b. expectancy theory.
    c. time and motion outcomes.
    d. coercive.

11. _____ is the range of skills used by officers in the achievement of objectives.
    a. Stated expectation
    b. Assigned valence
    c. Electronic competence
    d. Performance potential

12. An officer who has in increase in pay because of increased in arrest activity is said to have received an _____ reward.
    a. extrinsic
    b. intrinsic
    c. exemplary
    d. altruistic

13. Equity theory says that a person's motivation is affected by his/her perception of:
    a. fairness in the workplace.
    b. group motivations, not individual.
    c. dissatisfaction.
    d. the criminal justice system.

14. Theory Z suggests that organizations can no longer exist _____.
    a. privately   b. publically   c. in a social vacuum   d. democratically

15. This theory says that motivation is determined not only by organizations, but also by _____.
    a. police benefits.
    b. influences in society.
    c. judges and lawyers.
    d. administrations.

16. Proactive and flexible management strategies help insure the __ of employees.
    a. growth and maturity
    b. obedience to authority
    c. loyalty
    d. adherence to rules.

17. Brief, Munro and Aldag suggest the use of _____ for job enrichment in correctional institutions.
    a. pep talks
    b. quality circles
    c. large groups of managers
    d. court personnel

18. Angell first suggested that implementing _____ would greatly benefit policing.
    a. traditional police hierarchy.
    b. employee' rights committees
    c. Management by Objectives
    d. participatory management blockades

19. Which one of the following is not an element of an integrated model of motivation?
    a. personal motives and values
    b. reinforcement
    c. material resources
    d. lack of attention to individual needs

20. The goal of creating a motivational environment is to assure _____ by employees.
    a. maximum effort
    b. minimum stress
    c. more jobs
    d. major changes.

Appendix C - 15

Chapter 6
Job Design

1. In problem-oriented policing officers will support needed change because ____.
    a. more money is involved.
    b. more status.
    c. they are an essential part of it.
    d. they are ordered to.

2. In criminal justice, job design describes ____.
    a. deliberate, purposeful planning of a job.
    b. architects' models.
    c. theories.
    d. caseloads.

3. Which of these did Karl Marx not warn about concerning good jobs?
    a. impersonal work
    b. enough light in the workplace
    c. unfulfilling jobs
    d. developing physical and mental powers

4. The primary focus of Frederick Taylor's work concerned ____.
    a. variety.
    b. respect.
    c. elbowroom.
    d. efficiency.

5. Deprofessionalization syndrome refers to ____.
    a. a psychological state.
    b. decreased discretion.
    c. decreased control.
    d. accountability of management.

6. Standardized classification instruments tend to _____ the judgement of probation and parole officers in assessing their cases.
    a. restrict
    b. vilify
    c. enlarge
    d. accurately assess

7. How do educational levels of policy officers correlate with job satisfaction?
    a. they tend to stay longer on the job
    b. they tend to leave before retirement

c. they participate more willingly in training
  d. their attitudes are more positive all along

8. What did the Maslach Inventory measure among probation and parole officers?
   a. salary satisfaction
   b. status of workers
   c. opportunities for advancement
   d. burnout

9. Which of the following is not important for workers, according to the human relations school?
   a. leisure
   b. responsibility
   c. recognition
   d. opportunities for achievement and growth

10. A model of job enrichment based on research and individual differences was developed by
    a. Morse.
    b. Herzberg.
    c. Hackman and Oldham.
    d. Motivation theory.

11. The Job Diagnostic Survey measures the _____ of the job.
    a. core job dimensions
    b. technical dimensions
    c. time-motion studies
    d. descriptions

12. An important program by _____ disconfirms the idea that higher levels of the Maslow hierarchy are reserved for skilled workers.
    a. IBM
    b. General Motors
    c. Work in America
    d. Texas Instruments

13. Which one of the following is cited as the main reason for psychiatric aides staying on the job, according to Simpson and Simpson?
    a. job security
    b. intrinsically rewarding tasks
    c. pay
    d. fellow workers

14. Increasing responsibilities of front-line staff to enrich jobs is called ____.
    a. supervision.   b. overloading.   c. enlarging.   d. vertical loading.

15. Skolnick and Fyfe argue that police violence against citizens is tied to the _____ of police organizations.
    a. military structure
    b. democratic organization
    c. peer pressure
    d. confrontations

16. _____ is a model developed by Angell, which parallels autonomous work groups in industry.
    a. police hierarchy
    b. jail operation
    c. team policing
    d. cultural diversity

17. Which program was developed by the Federal Bureau of Prisons s an alternative to the traditional prison hierarchy?
    a. similar architecture
    b. grouping inmates in larger units
    c. unit management system
    d. conformity

18. Direct supervision of jail management encourages workers to ____.
    a. complain more to their supervisors.
    b. view their work more positively.
    c. develop more bureaucracy.
    d. keep their power for themselves.

19. The Community Resource Management Team has been developed as an alternative to the ____.
    a. traditional caseload model.
    b. idea of team policing.
    c. usual jail setting.
    d. more counseling.

20. Community policing creates a police department that is ____.
    a. more cohesive.
    b. more fragmented.
    c. more competitive.
    d. less communicative.

Chapter 7
Leadership

1. A process that effectively accomplishes organizational goals is called _____.
    a. coercion.
    b. leadership.
    c. accomplishment.
    d. purpose.

2. _____ are simple procedures to influence behaviors.
    a. Techniques
    b. Processes
    c. Styles
    d. Objectives

3. It must be understood that leadership is inherently _____ in public bureaucracies.
    a. dangerous
    b. corrupt
    c. simplistic
    d. political

4. Leadership is a process which is rooted in some type of _____.
    a. focus.
    b. agency.
    c. authority.
    d. quality.

5. Which one of the following is not included in the three approaches to theories of leadership described in research?
    a. the instincts or traits of the leader
    b. the external political environment
    c. the behavior of the leader
    d. multiple variables in the process of leadership

6. The behavioral models accentuate how leaders initiate _____ with subordinates to get them to accomplish organizational tasks.
    a. competition
    b. interaction
    c. identity
    d. concern

7. The Ohio State Studies examined leadership on two dimensions: _____ and initiating structure.
    a. consideration
    b. situation
    c. caution
    d. salesmanship

8. One of the limitations of the Ohio State Studies was that its only applicable to:
    a. managers.
    b. subordinates.
    c. broad concerns.
    d. specific situations.

9. The Michigan Studies dichotomized leadership into two concerns. One was:
    a. profit centered supervisors.
    b. personality centered supervisors.
    c. production centered supervisors.
    d. purpose centered supervisors.

10. One of the problems with the behavioral approach is that leadership may not be:
    a. enacted   b. Measured   c. effective   d. managed

11. _____ suggests that leadership research that has been done on private organizations may not apply to public ones.
    a. Construct validity
    b. Conceptual validity
    c. Extraneous validity
    d. External validity

12. Contingency theories of leadership emphasize the _____ within which leadership is expressed.
    a. contact
    b. corporation
    c. context
    d. communication

13. Which one of the following is not a constraint of Fiedler's Contingency Model?
    a. peer groups
    b. leader-member relations
    c. task structure
    d. position power

14. An unfavorable description of a co-worker denotes a _____ leadership orientation.
    a. human relations
    b. task production
    c. powerful
    d. psychological

15. One of the implications in Fiedler's Theory for criminal justice management calls for matching the right leader with _____ tasks.
    a. harder   b. less stressful   c. more varied   d. the right

16. According to Path Goal Theory leadership can be understood as a/an _____ between leader behavior and the situational aspects in an organization.
    a. stand-off
    b. dichotomy
    c. interaction
    d. effect

17. Which is not a style of leadership suggested by Path Goal Theory?
    a. nondirective
    b. supportive
    c. participative
    d. achievement-oriented

18. Locus of control, authoritarianism, and ability are all _____ characteristics.
    a. managerial
    b. subordinate
    c. performance
    d. external

19. One is not considered an environmental factor in the work situation:
    a. task.
    b. formal authority.
    c. informal authority.
    d. primary work group.

20. Some research on police indicates that a _____ task and _____ employee centered approach is preferred.
    a. high, high
    b. high, low
    c. low, high
    d. low, low

Chapter 8
Personnel Supervision and Evaluation

1. Most of the basic tenets of traditional supervision focused on _____ of performance.
    a. societal expectations
    b. hard measures
    c. organizational objectives
    d. personal goals

2. According to Stojkovic and Lovell, fundamental ways in which correctional administrators make decisions have to do with _____ .
    a. hard data
    b. multiple functions
    c. justification
    d. myths and symbols

3. _____ typically make up most crimes.
    a. Misdemeanors
    b. Felonies
    c. Crimes of passion
    d. Murders

4. For criminal justice administrators the central objective is to determine the goals of their _____ .
    a. employees.
    b. governing boards.
    c. communities.
    d. functions.

5. Which of the following is not a dimension of Hall's model of understanding organizational structure?
    a. centralization
    b. formalization
    c. evaluation
    d. complexity

6. _____ within police organizations has meant allowing greater autonomy and authority in decision-making among police employees.
    a. Differentiation
    b. Decentralization
    c. Diffusion
    d. Deployment

7. Goldstein suggests expanding the role of police supervisor and including a view of _____ as the primary goal of the department.
   a. problem-solving
   b. authority
   c. work ethics
   d. hierarchy

8. A significant change in the mid-1970's was the _____ and management philosophy of jail environments.
   a. economic base
   b. disciplinary problem
   c. architecture
   d. training

9. Formalization is a _____ for all criminal justice organizations.
   a. variable   b. goal   c. control   d. constant

10. Besides laws enacted by the federal government, other types of control over criminal justice organizations include _____ .
    a. monetary rewards.
    b. public interest groups.
    c. private sector bodies.
    d. public accountants.

11. Complexity of supervision refers to the _____ or _____ of an organization.
    a. width, length
    b. tallness, flatness
    c. depth, height
    d. openness, closeness

12. One of the following does not characterize the traditional model of employee supervision:
    a. creativity.
    b. centralization.
    c. formalization.
    d. complexity.

13. Span of control refers to the appropriate _____ of employees that can be managed by any one supervisor.
    a. type   b. cost   c. number   d. revelance

14. Unity of command's importance revolves around _____ orders from supervisors.
    a. single
    b. multiple and conflicting
    c. clear and concise
    d. situational

15. Delegation of authority maintains the integrity of the organization in the traditional model of supervision by clearly defining tasks and responsibilities of _____ .
    a. authority figures.
    b. community resources.
    c. employees.
    d. organizations.

16. To Fyfe it is not clear how the traditional model of police supervision is related to the _____ of police organizations.
    a. authority
    b. production
    c. motivation
    d. goals

17. Which model attempts to integrate employee goals into organizational goals?
    a. human service   b. community service   c. traditional   d. architectural

18. Employee ownership, delegation, and the sharing of power comprise a work philosophy known as
    a. management by objectives.
    b. time management.
    c. people skills.
    d. unit management.

19. Wilson names some possible problems to innovation in publica organizations. Which one of the following is not included in his list?
    a. accountability   b. analysis   c. equity   d. efficiency

20. The challenge facing criminal justice administrators will be how to be attention to the demands of _____ while remaining sensitive to other interests, goals, and constraints.
    a. the community
    b. bureaucracies
    c. employees
    d. researchers

Chapter 9
Group Behavior in Criminal Justice

1. A system of rules best describes _____, according to Katz and Kahn.
   a. organizations
   b. seasoning
   c. values
   d. socialization

2. Social control is a way to perpetuate _____ to the established culture.
   a. laws
   b. myths
   c. stories
   d. conformity

3. Which of these groups share the beliefs of the dominant culture?
   a. societies
   b. subcultures
   c. social service
   d. substantive

4. A primary mission of the criminal justice system does not include_____.
   a. controlling crime.
   b. creating social norms.
   c. determining justice.
   d. providing forms of social service.

5. Supervisory structures is one way that administrators can control the behavior of agency staff through _____.
   a. line staff.
   b. cultural variables.
   c. formal frames.
   d. hierarchy.

6. Which of the following determines stable behavior in organizations?
   a. deeply entrenched organizational culture
   b. individual personalities
   c. unpredictability
   d. dramatic changes in the environment

7. Role expectations are the standards by which the _____ of an organizational member is judged.
   a. qualifications

b. behavior
   c. anticipation
   d. values

8. Escalation episodes are described in a study by _____.
   a. Studt.
   b. common law wives.
   c. the New Judges Seminars.
   d. surveillance officers.

9. In criminal justice, which problem is discussed most often?
   a. taking on of new roles
   b. complying with rules
   c. rehabilitation of criminals
   d. conflict in roles

10. _____ aims at furthering the perceived goals of an organization, rather than providing benefits to an individual, such as corruption.
    a. maximum security
    b. disciplinary procedures
    c. official deviance
    d. uncertainty

11. Which is not an example of "good police material", according to Charles.
    a. extremely aggressive behavior
    b. accepting of authoritarian atmosphere
    c. wanting long-term (20 years or more) employment
    d. interested in fighting crime

12. The _____ is more elaborate in policing than any other criminal justice occupation.
    a. anticipatory socialization
    b. formal socialization
    c. informal socialization
    d. motivation

13. Van Maanen has identified a critical moment in training and initiation as _____.
    a. close encounter.
    b. probation.
    c. evaluation.
    d. enforcement encounter.

14. In 1970 in the Midwest, the informal socialization of the police officers supported _____ in the wake of public criticism.
    a. the use of violence
    b. prohibition
    c. openness with the media
    d. in-fighting

15. A significant reality shock happens to a rookie corrections officer when he/she:
    a. observes stereotypical behavior from inmates.
    b. encounters dangerous criminals.
    c. first has contact with inmates.
    d. enters the training academy.

16. In corrections, field training officer programs are usually _____ than police.
    a. more formal
    b. less formal
    c. more significant
    d. more social

17. The first corrections academy opened in _____.
    a. 1934
    b. 1960
    c. 1981
    d. 1859

18. _____ of occupational roles begins the socialization process.
    a. understanding
    b. designing
    c. influencing
    d. anticipation

19. Some authors have used the term _____ instead of subculture, referring to corrections officers.
    a. pluralistic ignorance
    b. suspicion
    c. custodial
    d. punitive

20. What is the term used for training new members as a group?
    a. formalization
    b. collective socialization
    c. strategy
    d. serial socialization

Chapter 10
Power and Political Behavior

1. There are different forms of _____ within the various components of the criminal justice system.
   a. relationship
   b. power
   c. organization
   d. bureaucracy

2. Dahl suggests that power is the ability to influence the _____ of another.
   a. emotions
   b. mental state
   c. status
   d. behavior

3. Power can be understood through an understanding of _____ of people and units.
   a. interactions
   b. opinions
   c. communication
   d. knowledge

4. What best describes substitutability?
   a. organizations can be changed
   b. organizations can be mediated
   c. organizations can be replaced
   d. organizations can be understood

5. Non-substitutable and central organizations tend to be very _____.
   a. stable.
   b. powerful.
   c. amenable.
   d. organized.

6. Over time, power becomes legitimized as _____.
   a. bureaucracy.
   b. supervision.
   c. authority.
   d. leadership.

7. Any discussion of the types of authority begins with _____.
   a. Weber   b. Emerson   c. Perrow   d. Hickson

8. One of the following is not included in the three types of authority:
   a. traditional
   b. charismatic
   c. legal
   d. coercive

9. The bases of power in all organizations is used to gain the _____ of subordinates.
   a. trust
   b. power
   c. compliance
   d. ear

10. The receiver of the power expression is the _____.
    a. power recipient.
    b. power holder.
    c. power wielder.
    d. power monitor.

11. Coercive base of power lies in the belief that there is some _____ if one does not do what one is told.
    a. reward
    b. punishment
    c. compliance
    d. reason

12. A legitimate power holder is able to influence a power recipient to do something based on some _____ of the power recipient.
    a. psychological need
    b. cognitive reason
    c. remuneration
    d. internalized belief

13. Which power has its base in identification?
    a. referent
    b. refused
    c. renewed
    d. reliable

14. _____ power is based on the power recipient's belief that the power holder has a high level of expertise in a subject area.
    a. Experiential   b. Exterior   c. Expert   d. Exact

15. Bacharach and Lawler refer to _____ as another form of power.
    a. ability
    b. informal rules
    c. control
    d. information

16. Still another kind of power refers to the ability to acquire and provide _____ to an organization.
    a. strong leadership
    b. needed resources
    c. law and order
    d. stability

17. Legitimate power is highly related to _____ functions, such as communication and coordination.
    a. communal
    b. legal
    c. leadership
    d. congruent

18. Which power is most highly related to facilitating evaluations and total functional behavior?
    a. coercive
    b. reward
    c. referent
    d. expert

19. Political behavior is a result of a lack of _____ among members about goals.
    a. means
    b. ends
    c. consensus
    d. conflict

20. Increased psychological dependent and psychological withdrawal characterize _____.
    a. resistance.
    b. learned helplessness.
    c. acceptance.
    d. rebellion.

Chapter 11
Organizational Conflict

1. Precursors to conflict, such as resource scarcity or policy differences in organizations, are_____ conditions of conflict.
    a. antithetical
    b. argumentative
    c. assertive
    d. antecedent

2. Conflict can produce _____ states within individuals in organizations.
    a. affective
    b. allied
    c. adversarial
    d. alternative

3. The perceptions of employees about their awareness of conflict in their organizations and to what degree it influences their behaviors are called _____ states.
    a. concealed
    b. concerned
    c. cognitive
    d. considered

4. What kind of conflict exists within the individual and usually involves some form of goal conflict or cognitive conflict?
    a. persevering
    b. perceptive
    c. protective
    d. personal

5. Conflict that occurs in organizations when individual members disagree on some point of common concern is called _____ conflict.
    a. interagency
    b. group
    c. organizational
    d. community

6. _____ conflict exists between those individuals who are in differing positions of authority within the organizational hierarchy.

    a. Vertical   b. Horizontal   c. Line-staff   d. Role

Appendix C - 31

7. When there is a common purpose among many disparate organizational units, yet disagreement as to how that purpose will be addressed, there occurs _____ conflict.
    a. intraorganizational
    b. interorganizational
    c. intramural
    d. intercepted

8. One of the following is not an example of latent conflict.
    a. competition for scarce resources
    b. drives for autonomy
    c. concerted action
    d. divergence of subunit goals

9. _____ conflict occurs when two individuals recognize that a conflict situation exists between them.
    a. Perceived
    b. Felt
    c. Manifest
    d. Psychological

10. If conflict continues, the conflict _____ may lead to more serious problems.
    a. resolution
    b. aftermath
    c. personification
    d. decision

11. _____ describes a conflict behavior in which the individual is willing to assert own concerns over the concerns of the other individual.
    a. Collaborating
    b. Compromising
    c. Cooperating
    d. Competing

12. Accommodating behavior seeks to _____ the concerns of the other individual over one's concerns in a conflict situation.
    a. Avoid   b. Nullify   c. Satisfy   d. belittle

13. Which statement describes the appropriateness of conflict behavior?
    a. It is relevant to the context.
    b. The avoiding style is bad.
    c. It is not situation-dependent.
    d. The middle ground is always best.

14. Consciousness-raising interventions attempt to change the _____ of the parties which shape their behavior.
    a. expectations
    b. internal experiences
    c. situations
    d. external pressures

15. In interaction management, the supervisor directly intervenes in the conflict situation between two of the following:
    a. coordinates
    b. administrators
    c. peers
    d. subordinates

16. Rules that people know yet are not written down are called _____ rules.
    a. Informal   b. Informative   c. Illegal   d. intervention

17. Concerns of two parties in an organization that are mutually incompatible are:
    a. personal characteristics.
    b. constituent pressures.
    c. conflicts of interests.
    d. power and status.

18. Selection interventions attempt to select the people who would be the most _____ to the organization and to the job.
    a. economical
    b. advantageous
    c. powerful
    d. forthright

19. Which of the following is a good result of conflict in the criminal justice system?
    a. change
    b. increased status
    c. decreased crime
    d. competition

20. The only way conflict management is going to be useful to criminal justice organizations is if _____ is increased both within and among the components.
    a. pay
    b. respect
    c. outcomes
    d. communication

Chapter 12
Decision Making in Criminal Justice

1. _____ are information processing standards governing how the elements of the decision are combined.
    a. Arbitration rules
    b. Decision rules
    c. Labor rules
    d. Combination rules

2. Most decisions are guided by a _____ or broad framework.
    a. guideline
    b. network
    c. theory
    d. manager

3. One of the following is not included in what a decision maker needs regarding information:
    a. alternatives
    b. consequences
    c. subject
    d. goals

4. Getting acceptable results rather than optimal results is called _____ in criminal justice.
    a. satisficing
    b. satisfying
    c. sacrificing
    d. sufficiency

5. A repertoire of responses with ready made answers is called a _____.
    a. dust bin.
    b. collection.
    c. screen.
    d. garbage can.

6. The _____ of decision making is a product of bounded rationality.
    a. success
    b. stability
    c. sureness
    d. sweetness

Appendix C - 34

7. The most important characteristic of _____ is its accuracy.
   a. information
   b. a decision
   c. structure
   d. an official file

8. Being highly predictable is a mark of _____ decisions.
   a. indiscrete
   b. doubtful
   c. discretionary
   d. insoluble

9. A problem with accuracy is the need to use _____ information about people.
   a. quality
   b. summary
   c. highly detailed
   d. widely disseminated

10. Knowing about an offender's past record is part of the _____ (Burnham).
    a. Doppler Effect
    b. media hype
    c. numerical scores
    d. order effect

11. Lipsky states that latitude in front-line staff's decision making is one of the _____ of human service organizations.
    a. biggest problems
    b. best-kept secret
    c. least reliable method
    d. defining characteristics

12. Newman argues that the discretionary process of plea bargaining can promote _____ by addressing the variability and complexity of offenses.
    a. fairness
    b. bitterness
    c. confusion
    d. anger

13. What process recognizes that sentencing is a complex process?
    a. the denial of discretion
    b. the uselessness of discretion
    c. the structuring of discretion
    d. the elimination of discretion

14. _____ methods use mathematical formulas to predict people's behavior.
    a. Clinical
    b. Statistical
    c. Psychological
    d. Personality assessment

15. Dangerousness, repeat offending, and failure on parole are descriptions of decisions based on _____.
    a. fact
    b. conjecture
    c. criterion
    d. bias

16. With statistical methods, _____ are the same for all cases.
    a. predictors
    b. crimes
    c. decisions
    d. variables

17. Base rate in criminal justice predictions is _____ by decision makers.
    a. always the same
    b. widely publicized
    c. never revealed
    d. frequently unknown

18. Equity refers to _____ in similar circumstances being treated in similarly.
    a. legal arguments
    b. moral imperatives
    c. similar offenders
    d. only men

19. What theory may require the arrest, prosecution and long sentences for only a few people?
    a. consistency theory
    b. deterrence theory
    c. accuracy theory
    d. resource theory

20. When possible, encourage _____ decisions, rather than individual.
    a. group
    b. bureaucratic
    c. sole
    d. Estimated

Chapter 13
Organizational Effectiveness

1. _____ is a key consideration in evaluating effectiveness.
    a. Complexity
    b. Comprehension
    c. Communication
    d. Control

2. One factor of effectiveness requires a degree of _____ between outcomes.
    a. organization
    b. purpose
    c. evaluation
    d. congruence

3. Concern with effectiveness can often lead to the _____ of resources within and across organizations.
    a. hoarding
    b. redistribution
    c. emphasizing
    d. downsizing

4. The perspective of dominant coalition reflects the interests of those _____.
    a. in most need.
    b. at the bottom.
    c. in power.
    d. most invested.

5. The case of Ruiz v. Estelle illustrates the importance of the question of which of the following:
    a. effectiveness-for-what.
    b. non-effectiveness.
    c. effectiveness-for-whom.
    d. the effect of violence.

6. Some theoretical perspective must underlie any discussion of _____, according to Hannan and Freeman.
    a. distribution
    b. success
    c. effectiveness
    d. failure

7. The goal model defines effectiveness as the degree to which an organization _____ its goals.
    a. realizes
    b. describes
    c. negates
    d. simplifies

8. Perrow distinguishes between _____ goals and operative goals.
    a. specific
    b. complex
    c. official
    d. characteristic

9. One problem with focusing on organizational goals relates to the consequences of measuring goal _____.
    a. purpose.
    b. attainment.
    c. reality.
    d. setters.

10. A model of examining organizational effectiveness that is consistent with the human relations perspective is the _____ model.
    a. external procedure
    b. comparable results
    c. identification
    d. internal process

11. The strategic-constituency model is not concerned with questions such as ___.
    a. money.
    b. management.
    c. morale.
    d. mobility.

12. One of the following is not a component of the process approach:
    a. goal optimization.
    b. systems view
    c. behavioral emphasis
    d. end state.

13. In the system-resource model, organizations not assumed to possess?
    a. Goals   b. Leadership   c. Stability   d. Outputs

14. A method known as _____ tries to examine causal links in the attainment of some goal.
    a. gross-malfunctioning analysis
    b. variable analysis
    c. revelatory analysis
    d. sophisticated analysis

15. Mastrofski and Wadman distinguish between performance _____ and performance measurement.
    a. appraisal
    b. recognition
    c. accomplishment
    d. tests

16. The selection of _____ is a significant step in the evaluation of effectiveness.
    a. behavior
    b. deterrence
    c. crime control
    d. domain of activity

17. A significant problem with the measurement of variables is the fact that choices made among measures may all be mathematically _____.
    a. slanted
    b. wrong
    c. correct
    d. computed

18. _____ is defined as the proportion of some specified group of offenders who fail, according to some criteria, within some specified time.
    a. Recalcitrance
    b. Relocation
    c. Rating
    d. Recividism

19. Which give a more comprehensive view of organizational effectiveness?
    a. single measures
    b. multigoal/multimeasure
    c. process measures
    d. structure measures

20. The four components of Skogan's logic model are intervention, context, mechanism, and _____.
    a. outcomes.   b. rewards.   c. effort.   d. program.

Chapter 14
Change and Innovation

1. Attempts to reform the criminal justice system began at least as early as _____ .
    a. the mid-1800s.
    b. the early 1800s.
    c. the late 1800s.
    d. the early 1900s.

2. Change will occur from _____ within the agency.
    a. cohesion
    b. consensus
    c. communication
    d. conflict

3. Organizations modify their internal workings to adapt to external _____ .
    a. perceived needs.
    b. computer crimes.
    c. environmental pressures.
    d. consequences.

4. Goodman and Kruke call _____ organization change a set of activities designed to change individuals, groups, and organization structure and process.
    a. pertinent
    b. planned
    c. performance
    d. behavioral

5. The need to identify present and future changes in an organization's mission is:
    a. motivation.
    b. vision.
    c. challenging.
    d. structural.

6. The identification of problems is crucial to planning and to avoiding the _____ approach to management.
    a. agency folklore
    b. traditional
    c. service aspect
    d. garbage-can

7. Rational planning requires that an agency's goals are _____ .
   a. contradictory
   b. dictatorial
   c. congruent
   d. deliberate

8. _____ is the human and more difficult aspect of planned change.
   a. Implementing change
   b. Avoiding change
   c. Assessing the need for change
   d. Creating obstacles to change

9. The role of the community police officer is viewed by many as being in conflict with their _____ role.
   a. Community   b. Traditional   c. Social   d. Personal

10. Organizations that typically have a high decentralization of power, low formalization, and high complexity are those that _____ facilitate change.
    a. never   b. rarely   c. readily   d. cannot

11. Toch and Klofas found that job satisfaction, especially among corrections officers, tends to be _____ .
    a. centralized.
    b. low.
    c. highly formalized.
    d. satisfactory.

12. Successful innovation within organizations depends in part on a positive correlation between external pressures for change and internally _____ change.
    a. prescribed need for
    b. strict adherence to
    c. perceived need for
    d. avoidance to

13. The larger the mass of people involved in the change process, the more implementation will be _____ .
    a. impeded.
    b. impacted.
    c. initiated.
    d. involved.

14. Major modifications may be required in the _____ of an organization in order to achieve desired change.
    a. perimeters
    b. number of employees
    c. work behaviors of members
    d. basic structure

15. Schein suggests that behaviors are largely a product of the organization's ___.
    a. economic base.
    b. culture.
    c. performance.
    d. constraints.

16. To increase the level of trust and support, to increase personal satisfaction, and to create an environment where authority is based on expertise are some of the objectives of
    a. personal development.
    b. goal development.
    c. organizational development.
    d. task development.

17. What is an example of a technique that attempts to get organizational members actively involved in the change process?
    a. studying policy and procedures manuals
    b. sensitivity training
    c. setting up traditional authority-oriented patterns
    d. reducing responsibilities of members

18. Social interventions fail when policy makers and planners fall into _____ traps, according to Sieber.
    a. Regressive   b. progressive   c. rendered   d. purposeful

19. An example cited by Decker and Doleschal of _____ criminal justice remedies was diversion programs that widened the criminal justice net.
    a. successful   b. cost-effective   c. offender's   d. fatal

20. Which is not included in Scolnick and Bayley's characteristics of police chiefs that are crucial to change and innovation in police agencies attempting to become crime prevention oriented:
    a. the chief must be more than an advocate of new programs.
    b. the chief must lie to people to accomplish goals.
    c. conscious efforts must be made to keep the new program in place.
    d. public support must be sought.

Chapter 15
Research in Criminal Justice Organizations

1. _____ was one of the contributions of the 1967 President's Commission on Law Enforcement and the Administration of Justice.
    a. Rational planning
    b. Fiscal responsibility
    c. Employees' rights
    d. Autonomy

2. In a class work in 1939, Robert Lynd asked the question, _____.
    a. "Information for Whom?"
    b. "What Role for Social Sciences?"
    c. "Public Policy When?"
    d. "Knowledge for What?"

3. Which of these researchers have not done work involving partnerships between researchers and practitioners?
    a. Fyfe and Sherman
    b. Frederick Taylor
    c. Todd Clear
    d. Toch and Jacobs

4. Lovell found there was little _____ use of research data in decision-making.
    a. instrumental
    b. symbolic
    c. conceptual
    d. coordinated

5. The most important source of information for managers is the word of _____.
    a. researchers
    b. journalists
    c. trusted colleagues
    d. editors

6. Practitioners and researchers may emphasize _____ of data.
    a. the same views
    b. different aspects
    c. the numbers
    d. published articles

7. One example of caution Elliot uses regarding academics' enthusiasm for influencing policy is the studies of police response to _____.

a. crime rates.
  b. inmate stays.
  c. domestic violence.
  d. recidivism.

8. The Minneapolis experiment was influential because it _____ policies that were already favored for other reasons.
  a. negated
  b. inflated
  c. collapsed
  d. supported

9. Opening up the _____ for critical examination is a major impact of taking research seriously.
  a. policy process
  b. prisons
  c. original findings
  d. objective analysis

10. Measures used in criminal justice research are least reliable at the _____.
  a. national level.
  b. statewide level.
  c. local level.
  d. confidence level.

11. _____ research refers to the development of the capacity within organizations to address their data and research needs.
  a. Out-house
  b. In-house
  c. Applied
  d. Controlled

12. Who was the founder of Total quality Management?
  a. Howard Carlson
  b. Toch and Grant
  c. Dr. W. Edwards Deming
  d. AT&T

13. In many agencies, a primary function of research may be to justify _____.
  a. program budgets.
  b. more research.
  c. less research.
  d. morale.

14. Top administrators often fail to _____ the research role to program managers.
    a. support   b. fund   c. acknowledge   d. clarify

15. Chin and Benne say that research assumptions about data contribute to _____ strategies for change.
    a. irrational
    b. rational-empirical
    c. researcher-practitioner
    d. available

16. Under power-coercive strategies, _____ is a source of coercive power.
    a. research
    b. assumption
    c. belief
    d. neutrality

17. In criminal justice, an example of outside groups using research to coerce change was which of the following?
    a. Kodak
    b. United Nations
    c. MADD
    d. General Motors

18. Normative-reeducative strategies emphasize that understanding is a/an _____ process.
    a. informational
    b. valued
    c. transactional
    d. educational

19. Kurt Levin coined the term _____ to describe normative reeducative strategies in the collection and analysis of data.
    a. basic research.
    b. consumer behavior
    c. expert analysis
    d. action research

20. _____ is enhanced by having members of an organization involved in research.
    a. Funding
    b. Meaningfulness
    c. Resistance
    d. Incompetence

Answer Key CHAPTER 1		Answer Key CHAPTER 2		Answer Key CHAPTER 3		Answer Key CHAPTER 4		Answer Key CHAPTER 5	
1.	B	1.	D	1.	B	1.	B	1.	B
2.	A	2.	C	2.	C	2.	D	2.	B
3.	C	3.	B	3.	A	3.	A	3.	C
4.	C	4.	C	4.	C	4.	B	4.	A
5.	B	5.	C	5.	A	5.	C	5.	D
6.	D	6.	A	6.	D	6.	A	6.	B
7.	B	7.	A	7.	D	7.	D	7.	C
8.	D	8.	B	8.	C	8.	B	8.	A
9.	A	9.	A	9.	A	9.	B	9.	D
10.	B	10.	C	10.	C	10.	A	10.	B
11.	D	11.	D	11.	D	11.	D	11.	D
12.	A	12.	A	12.	B	12.	A	12.	A
13.	D	13.	B	13.	A	13.	C	13.	A
14.	C	14.	D	14.	C	14.	B	14.	C
15.	C	15.	A	15.	A	15.	A	15.	B
16.	B	16.	C	16.	B	16.	B	16.	A
17.	C	17.	A	17.	D	17.	D	17.	B
18.	A	18.	D	18.	B	18.	C	18.	C
19.	A	19.	A	19.	C	19.	A	19.	D
20.	D	20.	B	20.	B	20.	B	20.	A

Answer Key CHAPTER 6		Answer Key CHAPTER 7		Answer Key CHAPTER 8		Answer Key CHAPTER 9		Answer Key CHAPTER 10	
1.	C	1.	B	1.	B	1.	A	1.	B
2.	A	2.	A	2.	D	2.	D	2.	D
3.	B	3.	D	3.	A	3.	B	3.	A
4.	D	4.	C	4.	C	4.	B	4.	C
5.	B	5.	B	5.	C	5.	C	5.	B
6.	A	6.	B	6.	B	6.	A	6.	C
7.	B	7.	A	7.	A	7.	B	7.	A
8.	D	8.	D	8.	C	8.	A	8.	D
9.	A	9.	C	9.	D	9.	D	9.	C
10.	C	10.	B	10.	B	10.	C	10.	A
11.	A	11.	D	11.	B	11.	A	11.	B
12.	D	12.	C	12.	A	12.	D	12.	D
13.	B	13.	A	13.	C	13.	B	13.	A
14.	D	14.	B	14.	B	14.	A	14.	C
15.	A	15.	D	15.	C	15.	C	15.	C
16.	C	16.	C	16.	D	16.	B	16.	B
17.	C	17.	D	17.	A	17.	D	17.	C
18.	B	18.	B	18.	D	18.	C	18.	A
19.	A	19.	C	19.	B	19.	A	19.	C
20.	A	20.	A	20.	C	20.	B	20.	B

Answer Key CHAPTER 11	Answer Key CHAPTER 12	Answer Key CHAPTER 13	Answer Key CHAPTER 14	Answer Key CHAPTER 15
1. D	1. B	1. A	1. A	1. A
2. A	2. C	2. D	2. D	2. D
3. C	3. D	3. B	3. C	3. B
4. D	4. A	4. C	4. B	4. A
5. B	5. D	5. D	5. B	5. C
6. A	6. B	6. C	6. D	6. B
7. B	7. A	7. A	7. C	7. C
8. C	8. C	8. C	8. A	8. D
9. A	9. B	9. B	9. B	9. A
10. B	10. D	10. D	10. C	10. C
11. D	11. D	11. C	11. B	11. B
12. C	12. A	12. D	12. C	12. C
13. A	13. C	13. A	13. A	13. A
14. B	14. B	14. B	14. D	14. D
15. D	15. C	15. A	15. B	15. B
16. A	16. A	16. D	16. C	16. A
17. C	17. D	17. C	17. B	17. C
18. B	18. C	18. D	18. A	18. C
19. A	19. B	19. B	19. D	19. D
20. D	20. A	20. A	20. C	20. B